IS JESUS A SOCIALIST?

What Jesus and the Bible Have to Say About Wealth and Poverty, Generosity and Greed, and Abundance and Scarcity

By Lee Habeeb

Is Jesus a Socialist? What Jesus and the Bible Have to Say About Wealth and Poverty, Generosity and Greed, and Abundance and Scarcity

Written by Lee Habeeb.

ISBN: 979-8-89317-301-7

Published by Grace & Favor™, a publishing imprint of Global Publishing Partners, LLC, Nashville, TN.

Printed in the USA.

25 26 27 28 29 30 31 32 33 34 USA 10 9 8 7 6 5 4 3 2 1

IS JESUS A SOCIALIST?

What Jesus and the Bible Have to Say About Wealth and Poverty, Generosity and Greed, and Abundance and Scarcity

CONTENTS

"THE MULTIPLICATION OF THE LOAVES AND FISHES"
BY GIOVANNI LANFRANCO, 1620–1625

INTRODUCTION

Christians around the world believe that God's Son walked the earth some 2,000 years ago. Jesus, the Bible teaches us, came to this world—our world—through a miraculous birth from a virgin named Mary, began His ministry when He was about 30 years old, and it ended approximately 3 years later with His crucifixion and death. A few days later, Jesus was resurrected from the dead, having died for all of our sins, past, present, and future.

He would be seen on at least eight occasions after His crucifixion, first by Mary Magdalene at the tomb (Mark 16:9), and last by as many as 500 followers, where He confirmed the completion of His mission on earth, after which His followers witnessed His ascension into heaven.

While He was here on earth—before and after His death—Jesus taught His followers about many things, among them compassion, faith, forgiveness, grace, mercy, and love. His mission on earth spoke to the personal life of mankind, not our political life. In fact, the biggest decision any Christian makes in his life is not, never has, and never will be, in a group. The most personal decision any of us make, accepting Jesus as our Lord and Savior, is done by each one of us alone, one person at a time. One heart at a time. One soul at a time.

Our Lord and Savior, Jesus, does not force us to follow Him. We must willingly volunteer for the job. Coercion was not a part of Jesus's teaching; love was the animating force of His ministry. After all, He walked this earth to understand and know us. And for us to know Him. For us to know He loves us so profoundly and unconditionally that He died for all of our sins, past, present, and future. That is a type of love that's hard for us as human beings to comprehend. But one thing is certain. Coercion and force are the opposite of Jesus's brand of love. And yet force and coercion are what drive modern socialist economies; the government compels its citizens living under socialism to help the needy and the poor. It is not done freely. Or voluntarily.

The fact of the matter is, Jesus's teachings had nothing to say about the nature and form that governments should take, but for the fact that we should:

> *"Render to Caesar the things that are Caesar's, and to God the things that are God's" (Mark 12:17 ESV; Matthew 22:21; Luke 20:25).*

This was Jesus's way of drawing a distinction between two kingdoms: the kingdom of this world, and the kingdom not of this world—and Jesus is the King of that world.

If Jesus had wanted to rule the earth, He surely could have, and gotten all the accolades and trappings of wealth and power. But in the 33 years Jesus walked the earth, He showed absolutely no desire or inclination to do so. Money and power were not His thing. How do we know? In Satan's final temptation, he took Jesus to a high mountain and showed Him all of the kingdoms of the world, and all the glory that went with it.

> *And he said to him, "All these I will give you, if you will fall down and worship me" (Matthew 4:9 ESV).*

But Jesus was not impressed by the offer.

> *"Be gone, Satan! For it is written, 'You shall worship the Lord your God and him only'" (Matthew 4:10 ESV).*

Jesus, we can safely say, did not walk the earth to run the affairs of state, or to become a worldly leader of men. His mission field was us—we human beings, all. And our hearts, souls, and minds. Those deeply individual and personal spaces—and those alone—were His preoccupation. From the time He walked the earth until now, Jesus has been concerned with our eternal and personal salvation, and with our hearts. Loving God was at the heart of Jesus's mission to the world, and loving us. He wanted those two things to be at the heart—and the center—of our lives, too.

But don't believe me. When one of the teachers of the law asked Jesus which of the commandments was the most important, Jesus answered:

> *"The most important one . . . is this: 'Hear, O Israel: The Lord our God, the Lord is one. Love the Lord your God with all your heart and with all your soul and with all your mind and with all your strength.' The second is this: 'Love your*

"MOSES WITH THE TEN COMMANDMENTS"
BY PHILIPPE DE CHAMPAIGNE, 1648

neighbor as yourself.' There is no commandment greater than these" (Mark 12:29-31 NIV).

Those were Jesus's top two commandments, so they must be ours as followers of Jesus. And loving our Lord is something we must do as individuals. Just as loving one another—loving our neighbors as ourselves—is something we must do as individuals. Governments don't love people. They can try to assist people, try to help people in need. But people love people. Individuals love other individuals. Love isn't a collective experience. It is a deeply personal one. It's the most powerful personal experience on earth. Life without love is inconceivable.

Yes, we can and should worship Jesus together and live and walk our Christian lives with groups of people, but we are called to love the Lord individually and personally. And we know from Scripture that He knows us all individually and personally. He knows our individual hearts and our minds better than we know our own.

If Jesus had wanted to end poverty in His time—or massively redistribute wealth—he didn't need to run for office or fashion a governing body or political system. He could have simply made those things happen. But He spent little time feeding the hungry—only a couple of occasions—and redistributing wealth. He fed the hungry masses most memorably at the mountain on the other side of the Sea of Galilee. But that story was less about feeding the hungry masses than letting the hungry masses witness for themselves—with their own eyes—who He was. Witness with their own eyes the miracles He could perform.

> *When the people saw the sign that he had done, they said, "This is indeed the Prophet who is to come into the world!" (John 6:14 ESV).*

As for wealth redistribution, Jesus never mentioned it or even hinted at it in the Bible. In one instance He was asked to play the role of equity judge and settle an outstanding claim over an inheritance, and Jesus quickly and curtly refused.

> *Someone in the crowd said to him, "Teacher, tell my brother to divide the family inheritance with me."*

> *Jesus replied, "Man, who appointed me a judge or an arbiter between you?" Then he said to them, "Watch out! Be on your guard against all kinds of greed; life does not consist in an abundance of possessions" (Luke 12:13-15 NIV).*

Jesus did not for even a second suggest any kind of redistribution or equal outcome. He instead warned those listening about the perils of greed, declining to be the busybody.

Which is why it seems so odd—indeed, so strange—to caricature Jesus, Our Lord and Savior, as the embodiment of a man-made political system like socialism. And so utterly odd to hear non-Christians, and some misguided Christians, call Jesus a socialist.

To reduce Jesus's life, death, and resurrection—and His profound teachings—to a mere political system is a mixture of folly and arrogance. And yet there are some people outside the Christian flock—and some inside it too—who believe that the life of Jesus, and His lessons and teachings, support the political and economic theory that has come to be known as socialism.

Before any real discussion can continue on the subject, it is first important to understand what the word *socialism* actually means. This is what *Dictionary.com* says:

> *Noun: a theory or system of social organization that advocates the ownership and control of the means of production and distribution, capital, land, etc., by the community as a whole, usually through a centralized government.*[1]

In short, socialism calls for no ownership of anything, from a private business to private property. And calls for a centralized government—a centralized authority—to control everything. In short, the state runs the lives of the people living in it, and it does so through the coercive power of the government. By force of law.

So what does the Bible have to say about socialism, if anything? What Scripture supports the idea that Jesus's teachings fall in line with modern-day socialism? This work will examine with great care what the Bible has to say about the matter. And what Jesus has to say in His own words. And with the help of His teaching, which often took the form of stories—or parables.

One thing is certain: anyone who believes that Jesus's message can be reduced—be shrunk down in size—to earthly realms like philosophy, ideology, or politics is reading a very different Bible than the rest of us.

> *"For my thoughts are not your thoughts, neither are your ways my ways," declares the Lord (Isaiah 55:8 NIV).*

This work will instead take a deep plunge into the many times and many ways Jesus talks about these things that consume mankind when it comes to our daily life around wealth—or the lack thereof. This work will cover a lot of ground—including wealth and poverty, property ownership and community ownership, free will and coercion, envy and greed—and last, scarcity and abundance. And with Jesus's teaching—and Scripture—as the backdrop.

The hope is that more pastors and more Christians spend time thinking and praying—and talking and teaching—about Jesus's call on our hearts when it comes to these all-important matters.

"CHRIST AND THE RICH YOUNG RULER"
BY HEINRICH HOFMANN, 1889

CHAPTER 1: DOES JESUS—DOES GOD—HATE MONEY AND WEALTH?

Let's cut to the chase; socialists use as their ammunition several stories in the Bible that seem to support their claim that Jesus hated wealth and money. That Jesus hated the rich. But is it true? What do those stories, many of which we know, really say and mean? Rather than talk about the stories, let's first examine them.

The first and most well-known verse about wealth is the story of the rich young man who approaches Jesus for advice. It appears in the Books of Matthew, Luke, and Mark. Here's the story as it appeared in the latter:

> *As Jesus started on his way, a man ran up to him and fell on his knees before him. "Good teacher," he asked, "what must I do to inherit eternal life?"*
>
> *"Why do you call me good?" Jesus answered. "No one is good—except God alone. You know the commandments: 'You shall not murder, you shall not commit adultery, you shall not steal, you shall not give false testimony, you shall not defraud, honor your father and mother.'"*

> *"Teacher," he declared, "all these I have kept since I was a boy."*
>
> *Jesus looked at him and loved him. "One thing you lack," he said. "Go, sell everything you have and give to the poor, and you will have treasure in heaven. Then come, follow me."*
>
> *At this the man's face fell. He went away sad, because he had great wealth (Mark 10:17-22 NIV).*

It is a remarkable story, one that starts with an important question good Christians—and even good people who are not Christians—have been asking from the beginning of time: "What must I do to inherit eternal life?"

Jesus asks the young man if he knows the commandments and then rattles off a bunch of them. The rich young man quickly replies that he's kept all of the commandments Jesus listed—and done so since he was a boy. This young man was no doubt a good guy—and a good Jew.

Before He gave the young rich man any further instruction, Jesus, according to Mark, "looked on him and loved him." What a powerful sentence:

> *Jesus looked at him and loved him (Mark 10:21a NIV).*

Jesus saw this young rich man for who he really was, as He sees all of us. And He loved him because the young man had an honest and sincere yearning to get to heaven. To be as good a man as he could be in Jesus's eyes.

But Jesus also knew that this young rich man had a strong attachment to his money. How did He know that? Because Jesus knows our hearts, and sees and knows what we can't. It is in this context—and out of love for the young rich man—that Jesus asks him to give up everything. To sell his possessions and give them to the poor.

> *"You will have treasure in heaven. Then come, follow me" (Mark 10:21b NIV).*

When the young man heard the instruction of Jesus, we learn that "his face fell," and that he "went away sad." He went away sad because he had *heard* Jesus's command, but could not *obey* Jesus's command.

It turned out that his love of his possessions—the comfort and security they provided—were too much to part with. His emotional attachment to his wealth and status overruled his willingness to follow the words of Jesus. Small wonder he "went away sad."

What was Jesus teaching the young man with this encounter? And why did He do it the way He did it? Jesus wanted to see if the young man loved his wealth more than God. Jesus wanted to see if the young man *worshipped* his wealth. If the young man had made a *false idol* out of his wealth. In short, Jesus wanted to see if the young man understood the all-important 1st two of the Ten Commandments:

> *1: You shall have no other gods before me.*
> *2: You shall not make for yourself an [idol] (Exodus 20:3-4a NIV).*

Remarkably, this wasn't just any man giving the rich young man advice. This wasn't any man testing the rich young man—and testing him not to trick him or harm him, but out of a deep love for him. And to give the young rich man some credit, he asked the right man for advice about how to gain eternal life. But he didn't like Jesus's answer. The young man could not give up his treasure, his wealth, and his money.

And deep down inside, he knew it was wrong. It's *why* he walked away sadly. He had just ignored Jesus's command. He chose his money over Jesus—his worldly possessions over eternity.

In each of our lives, we know that feeling. That feeling that comes over us when we know what God demands of us—what Jesus commands—and despite that, put something we treasure above Him. We are sad when that happens, if we have any kind of walk with Jesus, because we are convicted. We are sad because we know what we're doing is wrong, but our flesh gets the best of us. We choose our earthly kingdom—and desires of the flesh—over the eternal Kingdom.

It is in this context that Jesus looks around and says to His disciples the following memorable lines:

> *"Children, how hard it is to enter the kingdom of God! It is easier for a camel to go through the eye of a needle than for someone who is rich to enter the kingdom of God" (Mark 10:24-25 NIV).*

If the young rich man had worshipped his job more than the Lord, or worshipped an athlete, rock star, hobby, wife, or a pastor more than the Lord, the lesson of the story would have been the same. Jesus, in this story, is not condemning wealth; He is condemning the worship of wealth. To be more precise, He is questioning the young man's priorities. God wasn't first in the young rich man's life, and *that* was the point.

Jesus's purpose in asking the young rich man to give away his possessions was not to shame him, but to love him. The rich young man was challenged not for Jesus's sake, but for his own benefit. The fact of the matter is, we—all of us—are the ones who suffer when we put wealth or work or family or anything else over God. Because when we do so, we diminish and make smaller our relationship with God. The rich young man, in this way, is all of us. He is all of us when we misplace our priorities and don't put God first.

That's why reducing this complex and beautiful story to "Jesus hates wealth" is so awful. And so wrong. Because it reduces the sheer magnificence of Jesus's teachings to a crude political ideology.

Speaking of rich men in the Bible, it is Abraham (known as *Abram* until renamed by God in Genesis 17:5) who had the distinction of being the first rich man in Genesis.

> *Abram had become very wealthy in livestock and in silver and gold (Genesis 13:2 NIV).*

There was no prior reference to Abraham's wealth. We only know that he and his wife packed up their bags and took everything they owned and hit the road. He picked up and followed God's command to leave his homeland and journey to a land God would one day show him. God was asking this 75 year-old-man to take an epic road trip to a place unknown to him—and Abraham simply obeyed!

Being that Abraham was able to acquire possessions and servants in Haran, he was not a poor man when he left home. But he would end up not just wealthy, but as the Bible indicated, *very* wealthy. And all because of his obedience to God's command. His wealth would consist of more than material wealth. God also promised Abraham a large family filled with heirs. How large?

> *[The Lord] brought him outside and said, "Look now toward heaven, and count the stars if you are able to number them." And He said to him, "So shall your descendants be" (Genesis 15:5 NKJV).*

"JOB RESTORED TO PROSPERITY"
BY LAURENT DE LA HYRE, 1648

God in this story wants us to know that all true wealth, material, and other types too, come from Him. We do not need to strive to get wealth if we only will believe in Him and put Him first. And with the full understanding that God's vision for what constitutes wealth is far bigger and better than the materialistic version we mere mortals envision.

The fact of the matter is, the first rich man—the first materially wealthy man in the Bible—did what God asked him to do. Abraham did what the wealthy young man in the New Testament refused to do: put God first. And use God's blessing, his wealth, not to serve himself but to serve God.

TALES OF OTHER RICH MEN IN THE BIBLE

There were other rich men in the Bible as well. Job was one such man, a man God was deeply impressed with. Don't believe me? Here are God's own words to Satan about Job:

> *"Have you considered my servant Job? There is no one on earth like him; he is blameless and upright, a man who fears God and shuns evil" (Job 1:8 NKJV).*

You all know the story. Job was stripped by Satan of everything he cared about. And through his travails and his trials, Job persisted and did not lose his faith in God. By the end of the story, Job had come to a place where he had even managed to pray for his terrible friends, those three friends—Eliphaz, Bildad, and Zophar—who blamed Job for his losses. Those three friends judged Job and believed there must have been something he'd done to suffer such loss and grief. They did not know and could not have known that Job was going through what he was going through for precisely the opposite reason—it was *because* he was "blameless and upright" that he was experiencing such adversity. And yet his friends had no problem speaking on God's behalf, and judging him. Convicting him.

It would have been easy for Job to resent his friends—or even hate them. But Job's faith and obedience carried the day. Job instead chose to pray for his friends. And here's what happened afterward:

> *After Job had prayed for his friends, the LORD restored his fortunes and gave him twice as much as he had before. All his brothers and sisters and everyone who had known him before came and ate with him in his house. They comforted and consoled him over all the trouble the LORD had brought on him, and each one gave him a piece of silver and a gold ring.*
>
> *The LORD blessed the latter part of Job's life more than the former part. He had fourteen thousand sheep, six thousand camels, a thousand yoke of oxen and a thousand donkeys. And he also had seven sons and three daughters (Job 42:10-13 NIV).*

Wow! So much for God hating wealth. "The Lord blessed the latter part of Job's life more than the former part." God blessed Job's life with wealth, and not just material wealth—but with seven sons and three daughters, the precise number he'd lost as a result of Satan's attack.

There were even richer men in the Bible than Abraham and Job. Here was King David's obituary in the Bible:

> *Then he died at a good age, full of days, riches, and honor (1 Chronicles 29:28 ESV).*

David's son's wealth exceeded even his, and the Bible goes into great detail describing Solomon's material riches, riches that would make men like Bill Gates or Jeffrey Bezos look middle class. God blesses Solomon beyond any human's wildest dreams, but God also issued Solomon a warning.

> *"But if you or your descendants turn away from me and do not observe the commands and decrees I have given you and go off to serve other gods and worship them, then I will cut off Israel from the land I have given them and will reject this temple I have consecrated for my Name." (1 Kings 9:6-7 NIV)*

So how did this relationship begin? And where did these riches spring from? Recall that in 1 Kings 3, we learn of Solomon's love for the Lord, and it is in this chapter that God appeared to Solomon in a dream and said, "Ask what I shall give you" (1 Kings 3:5 ESV). God was giving Solomon a blank check to have anything he wanted. What did Solomon ask for? It wasn't, as most of us would have asked for, wealth or riches or protection or power.

> *"You have made your servant king in place of David, my father, although I am but a little child . . . And your servant is in the midst of your people whom you have chosen . . . Give your servant therefore an understanding mind to govern your people, that I may discern between good and evil" (1 Kings 3:7-9 ESV).*

Wow! Solomon could have asked for anything, but he humbled himself before the Lord and asked him for wisdom. We learn in verse 10 that Solomon's requests were pleasing to God, who had this to say:

> *"Behold, I now do according to your word. Behold, I give you a wise and discerning mind, so that none like you has been before you and none like you shall arise after you" (1 Kings 3:12 ESV).*

But God wasn't finished blessing Solomon.

> *"I give you also what you have not asked, both riches and honor, so that no other king shall compare with you, all your days. And if you will walk in my ways, keeping my statutes and my commandments, as your father David walked, then I will lengthen your days" (1 Kings 3:13-14 ESV).*

"DREAM OF SOLOMON"
BY LUCA GIORDANO , 1694–1695

What God was saying in the Old Testament to Solomon, Jesus would say too, again and again: "Seek me first. Put me first."

> *Seek first the kingdom of God and his righteousness, and all these things will be added to you (Matthew 6:33 ESV).*

And we know the rest of the story—King Solomon strayed from God's commands. In fact, he directly disobeyed God, who had warned him not to marry women from foreign nations, as they might cause him to worship their own gods. Solomon married them anyway, inspiring God's punishment:

> *So the LORD became angry with Solomon. Solomon had turned away from the LORD, Israel's God, who had appeared to Solomon twice. He had warned Solomon that he must not serve other gods. But Solomon did not obey the LORD's command. So the LORD said to Solomon, "I see the things that you have chosen to do. You have not obeyed my covenant and the laws that I commanded you to obey. So I will take the kingdom away from you" (1 Kings 11:9-11 EASY).*

It was women that got Solomon in trouble, not his wealth—or the pursuit of wealth. Actually, Solomon in all likelihood saw his many marriages as a way to strengthen his kingdom. It was more than likely that his desire to keep peace and preserve and expand his political power had more to do with Solomon's break from God than women themselves. Whatever Solomon's motivations—sexual or political, or some combination of the two—the Bible is pretty clear about what happened next.

As Solomon grew old, his wives turned his heart after other gods, and his heart was not fully devoted to the LORD *his God, as the heart of David his father had been (1 Kings 11:4 NIV).*

It makes no difference to Jesus whether you put money or women or work—or anything else—before God. One of Solomon's own proverbs says it best:

There is a way that seems right to a man, but its end is the way to death (Proverbs 14:12 ESV).

An important point must be made here. Nowhere in the Bible does putting God first mean that we will automatically attain wealth in

"SERMON ON THE MOUNT"
BY CARL BLOCH, 1877

the material sense of the word. That is nonsense. It is what some call "Prosperity Gospel," and it turns the worship of Jesus into some kind of TV game show where cash prizes get doled out to the winners. Jesus is not that kind of Savior.

When Jesus said "all things will be added to you," He did not guarantee that we would have great wealth or material possessions, but that we would no longer need to worry about the basic provisions of our life. Jesus wants us to trust the heavenly Father to provide for us—for His children—and trust in Him because we know He values us so greatly. Rather than worry, pursue Him. That's His message.

But we also learn from Scripture that material wealth isn't bad by itself. It is the love of money that's bad. Putting your riches and material possessions above God is the great sin. Worshipping wealth or possessions is the great sin—and a sin because it separates us from God.

What the rich young man did was put his material possessions above God. And that is something we are all capable of. And not just material possessions, but things that possess us. Things of this world that possess us. Many people put their work before God. Work, as we will learn later, is a godly thing, and an important thing—and something Scripture demands. It is when we put our work above God, when we worship our work, that we get into trouble. It can even be a home, a spouse, children. Or a good cause. And that's not counting the very bad things we can easily put before God—sexual things and drugs and alcohol. And lust for money and power, too, all of which when worshipped or abused can separate us from God.

Jesus's overriding message was that we can most certainly enjoy the blessings of the earthly world. But that we can't turn those blessings into false idols or false Gods. Jesus is very clear on this point:

> *"No one can serve two masters. Either you will hate the one and love the other, or you will be devoted to the one and despise the other. You cannot serve both God and money" (Matthew 6:24 NIV).*

Those words, part of His Sermon on the Mount, were clear about money; it can't rule your life. Jesus also said it was foolish to store up treasures on earth where "moths and vermin destroy and where thieves break in and steal" (Matthew 6:19) and urged us to instead store our treasure in heaven, where it will last forever. As Paul reminds us in Romans 6:16, a master is anything that enslaves us. It can be money, but also work, lust, sex, alcohol, status, and power. We cannot serve two masters, Jesus warns us, because we will inevitably end up hating one and loving the other. Because two masters demand two different sets of allegiance which will, sooner or later, come into conflict. The Lord is headed in one direction, and our flesh—and the world—are headed in the other.

Paul reminds believers that our old nature was crucified with Jesus on the cross so that we are no longer slaves of sin. In a very practical way, Paul shows us how to stop letting sin reign in our lives by comparing being a slave of sin to being a slave of God. There is good and bad news in this message, and here's the bad news first: we are all slaves. The good news is that we get to choose our master.

Here is one thing we know for certain: not once is there any attempt by Jesus or God to play class warfare among and between human beings. What Jesus—what the Bible—routinely challenges all of us to do, rich and poor and middle class too, is to put our own house in proper order. Our own life in order. Our own priorities in order. Our own hearts in order.

Jesus spoke of this simple and profound truth:

> *"For where your treasure is, there your heart will be also" (Matthew 6:21 NIV).*

The admonitions in the Bible against wealth were in fact admonitions against lives and hearts that are out of order. That are not focusing first and foremost on God.

THE MONEY CHANGERS IN THE TEMPLE: THE STORY BEHIND THE STORY

Another favorite Bible story used by people who believe Jesus was a socialist is the story of the money changers in the temple. This story is worth a look.

> *And Jesus entered the temple and drove out all who sold and bought in the temple, and he overturned the tables of the money-changers and the seats of those who sold pigeons. He said to them, "It is written, 'My house shall be called a house of prayer,' but you make it a den of robbers" (Matthew 21:12-13 ESV).*

It was almost the time for the Jewish Passover, as we learn in John 2:13-15. Jesus went to Jerusalem and upon arriving in the temple courts He found people selling cattle, sheep, and doves and others sitting at tables exchanging money. So mad was Jesus, we learned in John's account, that He "made a whip out of cords, and drove all from the temple courts" (John 2:15).

Jesus was justly angered at what He saw taking place in a sacred space that was set aside from the world. He rightly saw the rank com-

"CHRIST DRIVING THE MONEY CHANGERS FROM THE TEMPLE"
BY EL GRECO , 1570

mercial activity taking place in the temple as corrupting the holiness of the place—and we must always remember that holiness means "to be set apart."

One commentator, D. A. Carson, explained it best.

> *Instead of solemn dignity and the murmur of prayer, there is the bellowing of cattle and the bleating of sheep. Instead of brokenness and contrition, holy adoration and prolonged petition, there is noisy commerce.*[2]

Jesus was angry not because trading and money lending was happening. He was angry at *where* it was happening. It was the *location* of the activity that Jesus had a problem with, not the trading or lending. And He was also angry with *why* the trading was taking place. The selling of sacrifices angered Jesus, and the profits being made from *selling* those sacrifices.

In fact, not once in the Bible does God or Jesus condemn trading or bartering, as it was the way so much commerce happened back in those ancient times. It was the way life happened—the way life should be lived. Not once does Jesus drive money lenders out of a bank or any other commercial trading place. Because Jesus understood that coins allowed people to exchange their goods and services. To bring value to their work and common sets of measure. To live and survive and even thrive.

THE WEALTH STORY IN THE BIBLE STORY SOCIALISTS HATE

A story in the Bible that socialists absolutely deplore is the Parable of the Talents (Matthew 25:14-30). Socialists and those who make the claim that Jesus hated money and wealth avoid this passage, or pretend the passage doesn't exist, that's how much they wish this story wasn't told by Jesus. That's how much they hate this story. But tell it, Jesus did. Why He told it we will unpack in a bit. But let's go through the entire story and read it aloud—because it is that important.

The story Jesus tells begins with a man going on a long trip. Before departing, he calls his servants together and entrusts them with his property. He entrusts them with his money—his "talents," as money was measured and called in the day—while he was gone.

> *"For it will be like a man going on a journey, who called his servants and entrusted to them his property. To one he gave five talents, to another two, to another one, to each according to his ability. Then he went away. He who had received the five talents went at once and traded with them, and he made five talents more. So also he who had the two talents made two talents more. But he who had received the one talent went and dug in the ground and hid his master's money. Now after a long time the master of those servants came and settled accounts with them.*
>
> *And he who had received the five talents came forward, bringing five talents more, saying, 'Master, you delivered to me five talents; here, I have made five talents more.'*
>
> *His master said to him, "Well done, good and faithful servant. You have been faithful over a little; I will set you over much. Enter into the joy of your master.'*
>
> *And he also who had the two talents came forward, saying, 'Master, you delivered to me two talents; here, I have made two talents more.'*

His master said to him, 'Well done, good and faithful servant. You have been faithful over a little; I will set you over much. Enter into the joy of your master.'

He also who had received the one talent came forward, saying, 'Master, I knew you to be a hard man, reaping where you did not sow, and gathering where you scattered no seed, so I was afraid, and I went and hid your talent in the ground. Here, you have what is yours.'

But his master answered him, 'You wicked and slothful servant! You knew that I reap where I have not sown and gather where I scattered no seed? Then you ought to have invested my money with the bankers, and at my coming I should have received what was my own with interest. So take the talent from him and give it to him who has the ten talents. For to everyone who has will more be given, and he will have an abundance. But from the one who has not, even what he has will be taken away. And cast the worthless servant into the outer darkness. In that place there will be weeping and gnashing of teeth'" (Matthew 25:14-30 ESV).

What a story! Now it's time to unpack it. Notice to start that he did not give the three men equal amounts of talents. That at first glance seemed really unfair! And worse, that unequal distribution of talents by the master—from an ordinary human view—might set the three servants against one another. That unfair and unequal distribution of the master might create resentment among and between the servants. And a resentment toward the master, too.

But Jesus explains why the master did what he did. They were given the differing quantities of talents, Jesus noted, "each according to his ability." In short, when it came to managing money, when it came to the stewardship of money, he believed the men had differing abilities.

Note also that the master in the story did not use the word *invest* but the word *entrust*. He entrusted these men with his wealth. What two of them properly decided to do was invest—to the best of their abilities—their master's wealth. And for the master's sake, not their own.

The men used their God-given ability to increase what they'd been given for their master. Not to use it for themselves or consume it—to go on some kind of spending or shopping spree—but to grow what the master had given them.

The story gets really interesting when the master of the servants returns after his long trip away from home to settle accounts with the three men. The first two men report that they'd doubled the master's money, and to both men, the master has the same words:

"THE PARABLE OF THE TALENTS OR MINAS"
BY WILLEM DE POORTER, 17TH CENTURY

"'Well done, good and faithful servant. You have been faithful over a little; I will set you over much. Enter into the joy of your master'" (Matthew 25:21, 23 ESV).

If Jesus hated money and wealth, or money properly invested to make more money, He shows no such animosity for it in this story. Because the hearts of each of these men were fixed on their master, and not themselves.

But things get even more interesting when the third man approaches his master. Notice how he starts, because it starts with the man judging his master. It starts with his harsh words toward his master for some unperceived grievance or slight:

"'Master, I knew you to be a hard man, reaping where you did not sow, and gathering where you scattered no seed"' (Matthew 25:24 ESV).

This is not the way to impress a boss, for sure, telling him that he's a "hard man." It is certainly no way to impress our true Master, Jesus. We know men and women like this who gripe endlessly about their lot in life, about life's unfairness—and God's unfairness because some seem to have more of this or that than others. More money. More love. More friendships. More family. More joy. More and better health.

After insulting his master, the third man explains why he dug a hole in the ground and hid his master's money:

"'I was afraid, and I went and hid your talent in the ground"' (Matthew 25:25 ESV).

Fear drove the third man to bury his master's money. And fear, as we know, is Satan's purview, not the Lord's. Passage after passage in the Bible deals with the spirit of fear.

> *For God has not given us a spirit of fear, but of power and of love and a sound mind (2 Timothy 1:7 NKJV).*

> *"Let not your hearts be troubled, neither let them be afraid" (John 14:27 ESV).*

> *Cast your anxiety on him because he cares for you (1 Peter 5:7 NIV).*

> *Fear not, for I am with you; be not dismayed, for I am your God. I will strengthen you, I will help you (Isaiah 41:10 ESV).*

And this may be the best of all the passages about fear, and how it relates to the third man:

> *There is no fear in love. But perfect love drives out fear, because fear has to do with punishment. The one who fears is not made perfect in love (1 John 4:18 NIV).*

The third man did what he did out of fear, and he acted out of fear because he did not properly love his master as the other two men had done. The other two men risked losing their master's money because the alternative—to hide his money in the ground—was worse. And worse because it was fear based. The first two men did not fear their master, they loved him. The third man feared his master for precisely the opposite reason: because he didn't love him.

The master was not pleased with his servant's effort, or the reasons for his poor showing. And this is where the story gets really interesting, because the master really comes down hard on the third man. And again, this is Jesus Himself telling this story. The master calls the third servant a "wicked and slothful servant," and from there, it gets worse:

> *"'Then you ought to have invested my money with the bankers'" (Matthew 25:27 ESV).*

The master is basically saying, "If you distrusted me so much, why not at least get some interest on it?" But so hateful and bitter were the feelings of the third man toward the master, and he was filled with so much fear, that the man didn't even bother to put the money in a bank to get some interest on it.

Then came the final verdict from the master in Jesus's story, and this is why socialists and critics of inequality of wealth outcomes truly hate this Scripture. Because it actually increases wealth inequality between and among these three men, not decreases it.

> *"So take the talent from him and give it to him who has the ten talents. For to everyone who has will more be given, and he will have an abundance. But from the one who has not, even what he has will be taken away. And cast the worthless servant into the outer darkness. In that place there will be weeping and gnashing of teeth" (Matthew 25:28-30 ESV).*

Why did Jesus tell this story? And what can we learn from it? For starters, God has blessed all of us with different talents. He has created all of us differently and uniquely. In short, God recognizes our individual uniqueness and circumstance. He wants us to understand that too. When we compare our talents—our circumstances to others and our talents or wealth or anything else to others—envy is the inevitable and ugly outcome. And we know what Jesus—and what the Bible—says about envy.

The flip side of envy is a false sense of entitlement, and this story addresses that as well. Notice that the man who received five talents didn't think he was superior to the other two men. He had three more talents than the second man, and four more talents than the third. He could easily have concluded that he somehow deserved those talents, that he was somehow better than those other two men—and that they were his to use or spend freely on himself. But he did nothing of the sort, and put those five talents to work for his master. And his master was pleased. Pleased that his servant served the master's talents—served the master's money and property—instead of the other way around: have that master's money serve his servant.

The most interesting of the three men, for this discussion, is the second servant. He isn't bitter because he got a lot less than the first guy—more than 50 percent less. He doesn't gripe or complain. And he doesn't judge his master harshly, either. He doesn't call his master a "hard man" for giving him less and isn't afraid to invest the master's money as the third man was.

He instead takes what his master gave him, and does his very best with it, just as the first servant did. And like the first servant, he doubles his master's money. In short, he does not let what he does not have get in the way of doing the best with what he does have. He does the best with what God has blessed him with. He was grateful for what he *did* have, rather than ungrateful for what he didn't.

A focus on the unequal treatment of his master would have had the opposite effect on the second servant. Which is why his story is perhaps the most important of the three servants.

What this story reveals is this: when we think about inequality in the earthly realm, rather than God's realm, we can easily get in trouble. God Himself created us unequally in our talents, but He loves us equally. And uniquely. Our work on earth is to keep our eyes on Him. And love our neighbors, not compete against them—or compare ourselves and our lives to theirs.

We also learn from this story that if we don't properly use our talents, we can lose them. This is a part of the story that doesn't seem very Christlike at first glance.

> *"For to everyone who has will more be given, and he will have an abundance. But from the one who has not, even what he has will be taken away" (Matthew 25:29 ESV).*

Jesus's words here sound harsh but reveal a truth we all know and understand from real life experience. If you stop exercising for a long time, you lose your endurance. If you don't keep up with a foreign language, you lose it. We all know we can lose friendships over time if we don't nurture them. The fact is, Satan wants to rob us of our talents—the talents God poured into us—using fear, envy, laziness, idleness, and every other conceivable sin. Our job is to be good stewards of the talents God has blessed each and every one of us with.

"THE GOOD SAMARITAN"
BY REMBRANDT, 1633

CHAPTER 2: HELPING THE POOR BY CHOICE OR COERCION? LOVE OR COMPULSION?

Once again, as we did with the chapter on wealth, let's cut to the chase on the question of poverty and what Jesus expected of us when it came to helping the poor. It's a line that has been used and abused by Christians and non-Christians alike to indicate Jesus's stand on poverty:

> *"You will always have the poor among you, but you will not always have me" (John 12:8 NIV).*

Jesus says it clearly; poor people will always be here on earth and be here because He said so. He didn't say poor people will always be with us until we human beings end poverty everywhere in the world for all time. That wasn't His command to us. It was to help the poor, not end poverty. If Jesus had really wanted to eliminate poverty in His time, let alone ours, He most certainly could have. He was, after all, Jesus.

So what was Jesus up to when He said the poor will always be with us? And again, I emphasize the word *always*. This one line—and one word—has been used by some to absolve themselves of any responsibility to help the poor because they believe poverty is inevitable, so why bother to help? That's wrong, and tragically so, biblically speaking.

Others use the line to push for massive wealth redistribution plans through government action to eradicate poverty. Those people are wrong as well, and tragically so, biblically speaking.

It's important to look at Jesus's famous and often quoted line about the poor in its full context. Here it is—this one is also worth reading aloud:

"THE OINTMENT OF THE MAGDALENE"
BY JAMES TISSOT, 1900

> *Six days before the Passover, Jesus came to Bethany, where Lazarus lived, whom Jesus had raised from the dead. Here a dinner was given in Jesus's honor. Martha served, while Lazarus was among those reclining at the table with him. Then Mary took about a pint of pure nard, an expensive perfume; she poured it on Jesus' feet and wiped his feet with her hair. And the house was filled with the fragrance of the perfume.*
>
> *But one of his disciples, Judas Iscariot, who was later to betray him, objected, "Why wasn't this perfume sold and the money given to the poor? It was worth a year's wages." He did not say this because he cared about the poor but because he was a thief; as keeper of the money bag, he used to help himself to what was put into it.*
>
> *"Leave her alone," Jesus replied. "It was intended that she should save this perfume for the day of my burial. You will always have the poor among you, but you will not always have me" (John 12:1-8 NIV).*

What a story! And there is nothing simple about it. No simple or easy lesson can be drawn from it, except this: Jesus loves it when we genuinely and voluntarily give of ourselves, and from the depths of our heart.

The story starts with a big dinner to honor Jesus, who had come to Bethany and raised Lazarus from the dead. Speaking of miracles, Lazarus himself was among those at the dinner table partaking of the feast.

Mary decides to honor Jesus by taking care of His worn-out and weary feet, which was a sign of submission and servitude. Jesus's feet are not covered with socks and padded hiking boots; they are not today's pampered feet, for sure. But that doesn't stop Mary from pouring her perfume on them. It's not just any perfume she poured on Jesus's feet; it's *expensive* perfume. Perfume, as we learn from Judas, worth a year's wages.

After pouring her expensive perfume on Jesus's feet, she proceeds to wipe His feet with her hair. Her hair! Talk about an act of servitude and submission!

Then comes the angry reaction of Judas:

> *"Why wasn't this perfume sold and given to the poor?" (John 12:5 NIV).*

Judas asks this, rebuking Mary and letting everyone at the dinner know the actual value of the perfume he believes she is wasting on Jesus's feet. But as quickly as Judas rebukes Mary, Jesus rebukes Judas:

> *"Leave her alone. . . . It was intended that she should save this perfume for the day of my burial" (John 12:7 NIV).*

"Leave her alone!" Jesus says to Judas in front of a crowd. Ouch! Why does Jesus call out *Judas* so quickly? What does He know about the situation—and about Judas *and* Mary—that the people watching didn't know, or couldn't?

It's simple; Jesus knew Judas's *heart*. And He knew Mary's *heart* too. He knew that Mary was not showing off with her display of generosity, that she was neither prideful when she made her offering to Jesus nor wasteful. Jesus knew Mary's desire to please Him came from a good and virtuous place. Jesus also knew Judas's heart. Though Judas claimed he was scolding Mary for squandering a precious and valuable resource, Jesus knew Judas's real intent. He knew Judas was

"JESUS AND JUDAS"
BY GIOTTO, 1304

pretending to care about the poor and using it to take from the poor. Jesus knew Judas was a thief who filled his bags with money *meant* for the poor.

And He knew these things about Mary and Judas because He was Jesus! He knew their hearts. He knows our hearts, too. That's what this story was *really* about. Our hearts.

Jesus knows when we give generously. He knows when we give to show off, or out of pride. He knows those of us who claim to *care* about the poor, but don't actually give our own precious resources to the poor: our money and our time. Jesus knows the people who claim to help the poor—and who steal from the poor, too. He also knows the people who use their professed concern about the poor to gain power, and to even keep the poor mired in their poverty. And He knows when we don't give anything at all to the poor, not in words, thoughts, or deeds. He knows all of this.

It was in this context that Jesus ends His short teaching with the famous and often quoted line, "the poor you will always have with you."

Jesus was quoting from Scripture when He uttered that line, which people might have known from the Torah, and what would become the Old Testament:

> *"If among you, one of your brothers should become poor, in any of your towns within your land that the LORD your God is giving you, you shall not harden your heart or shut your hand against your poor brother, but you shall open your hand to him and lend him sufficient for his need, whatever it may be...For there will never cease to be poor in the land. Therefore I command you, 'You shall open wide your hand to your brother, to the needy and to the poor, in your land'" (Deuteronomy 15:7-8, 11 ESV).*

Throughout the Bible are such calls, and through the ministry of Jesus Himself. He commands us to serve the poor and needy voluntarily, joyfully, and cheerfully. But nowhere—not in one single instance—does Jesus ask that we force anyone or compel anyone to help the poor. Force and coercion, it must be repeated again and again, were not Jesus's way. Voluntary and joyful giving, with the right heart and intent, is Jesus's way. Love, not force and compulsion, is Jesus's way.

JESUS WASN'T BORN RICH

We must always remember the circumstances of Jesus's youth. He was, after all, born in a manger, which is another way of saying He was born in a barn! His adoptive father was a common carpenter, and at His purification ceremony, His parents were so poor they couldn't afford a sheep for the sacrifice, so they offered up much less expensive turtledoves—or pigeons.

We know from Scripture that Jesus loved the poor, but we must always remember that He lived among the poor His whole life. He also spent much of His time—especially during His ministry—with the wealthy. He stayed in their houses and blessed them, and they blessed Him and others with their generosity. Jesus even spent time with tax collectors and wealthy pharisees, and condemned some of them, not because they possessed wealth, but because their wealth possessed them.

Perhaps the best of all the stories in the Bible about the command to give to the poor is the story of the Tithing Widow in the Book of Mark:

> *Jesus sat down opposite the place where the offerings were put and watched the crowd putting their money into*

> *the temple treasury. Many rich threw in large amounts. But a poor widow came and put in two very small copper coins, worth only a few cents.*
>
> *Calling his disciples to him, Jesus said, "Truly I tell you, this poor widow has put more into the treasury than all the others. They all gave out of their wealth; but she, out of her poverty, put in everything—all she had to live on" (Mark 12:41-44 NIV).*

Notice first in this story that the obligation to serve the poor is one that applies to *all* of us, not just the wealthy. The poor widow in the story did not exclude herself from the command to give. She gave to the needy, as Jesus pointed out, more generously as a proportion of her wealth than even her most wealthy peers. Her sacrifice was greater in the eyes of Jesus. Her heart for the poor was greater. Her heart for the Lord was too.

"THE WIDOW'S MITE"
BY JAMES TISSOT, 1850

This story points to a crucial biblical theme: every man, woman, and child has something to give. We can *all* serve or help the poorest and most physically disabled among us.

Here is another case where Jesus teaches us about His heart for the poor, no matter our circumstance, rich or poor, clean or unclean. It is what is inside—what's in our hearts—that matters to Jesus. If our hearts are right, we will give to the poor and help the poor for the right reasons.

Here is another episode in which Jesus teaches on a similar theme: appearances vs. reality. It is the scene in the Bible where Jesus chastises the Pharisees for their worry about rules and outside appearances rather than what's inside us, in our hearts:

> *When Jesus had finished speaking, a Pharisee invited him to eat with him; so he went in and reclined at the table. But the Pharisee was surprised when he noticed that Jesus did not first wash before the meal.*
>
> *Then the Lord said to him, "Now then, you Pharisees clean the outside of the cup and dish, but inside you are full of greed and wickedness. You foolish people! Did not the one who made the outside make the inside also? But now as for what is inside you—be generous to the poor, and everything will be clean for you" (Luke 11:37-41 NIV).*

Time and again, we hear from Jesus when it comes to helping the poor. Repeatedly, He rebukes people, not for having wealth itself, but for having bad hearts like the Pharisees in the above passage who were trying to disqualify Jesus as a legitimate rabbi because He was not following the "correct" hygiene laws and protocols of Judaism.

Jesus wasn't concerned about such things. He doesn't care about outward appearances or our cultural and political status—and He

"THE SUPPER AT EMMAUS"
BY REMBRANDT, 1648

certainly doesn't care if we are rich, middle class, or poor. He cares about our heart for those around us in need, and for Him. This is crucial and can't be repeated enough. He knows our hearts. And we reveal our hearts for Him and for our neighbors—especially those who are needy and poor—when we serve them, when we love them, and when we share our wealth or time with them.

THE GOOD SAMARITAN: A STORY OF VOLUNTARY LOVE

One of the great stories in the Bible is the Parable of the Good Samaritan, a story worth reading in its entirety, beginning to end. Because Jesus told the story for a reason. Always, Jesus told stories for a reason. It is our work to discern what He was teaching us.

> *On one occasion an expert in the law stood up to test Jesus. "Teacher," he asked, "what must I do to inherit eternal life?"*
>
> *"What is written in the Law?" he replied. "How do you read it?"*
>
> *He answered, "Love the Lord your God with all your heart and with all your soul and with all your strength and with all your mind" and, "Love your neighbor as yourself."*
>
> *"You have answered correctly," Jesus replied. "Do this and you will live."*
>
> *But he wanted to justify himself, so he asked Jesus, "And who is my neighbor?"*
>
> *In reply Jesus said: "A man was going down from Jerusalem to Jericho, when he was attacked by robbers. They stripped him of his clothes, beat him and went away, leaving him half dead.*

> *A priest happened to be going down the same road, and when he saw the man, he passed by on the other side. So too, a Levite, when he came to the place and saw him, passed by on the other side. But a Samaritan, as he traveled, came where the man was; and when he saw him, he took pity on him. He went to him and bandaged his wounds, pouring on oil and wine. Then he put the man on his own donkey, brought him to an inn and took care of him. The next day he took out two denarii and gave them to the innkeeper. 'Look after him,' he said, 'and when I return, I will reimburse you for any extra expense you may have.'"*
>
> *"Which of these three do you think was a neighbor to the man who fell into the hands of robbers?"*
>
> *The expert in the law replied, "The one who had mercy on him.'"*
>
> *Jesus told him, "Go and do likewise" (Luke 10:25-37 NIV).*

What a story! And what a start to the story. The expert in law—the Pharisee—asks Jesus the very same question the rich, young man asked Jesus:

> *"How do I inherit eternal life?"*

Jesus did what He did best, which is answer the question with a question of His own. The legal expert answered it correctly: the way to eternal life is written in the law, which asks that we love God with all our heart, soul, and mind, and love our neighbors as ourselves. This has been the correct answer to followers of Jesus ever since.

And then came the next and trickier question from the Pharisee to Jesus:

> *"And who is my neighbor?"*

"THE GOOD SAMARITAN"
BY BALTHASAR VAN CORTBEMDE, 1647

It is in this context that Jesus answers that question with the story of the Good Samaritan.

Notice first that the Samaritan took pity on the beaten man on the side of the road. He felt compassion for him, but that feeling alone would not have made the story what it was. It was the actions of the Good Samaritan that made this story so powerful. These actions were no doubt stirred by his compassion—but he acted. He provided care and healing for the injured stranger, and also provided transportation and lodging, even going so far as to pay the innkeeper the next day. In short, the Good Samaritan went all in to care for a total stranger.

His heart was all in, and so was his mind, spirit, and body. He acted on his compassion and committed to helping a total stranger in need. This reveals a profound message within this story. The definition of a "neighbor" is very broad to Jesus. It is not simply your next-door neighbor He commands us to love, or a member of your church, or your group of friends, or your community.

Notice also that in the story, *two* men passed up the man in need on the side of the road. In his very last speech before he was assassinated in Memphis, Tennessee, in 1968, the Reverend Dr. Martin Luther King Jr. gave his take on those two men, and why they didn't stop, but the third man did.

> *It's possible that those men were afraid. You see, the Jericho road is a dangerous road. I remember when Mrs. King and I were first in Jerusalem. We rented a car and drove from Jerusalem down to Jericho. And as soon as we got on that road, I said to my wife, "I can see why Jesus used this as the setting for his parable." It's a winding, meandering road. It's really conducive for ambushing. You start out in Jerusalem, which is about twelve*

hundred miles, or rather, twelve hundred feet above sea level. And by the time you get down to Jericho, fifteen or twenty minutes later, you're about twenty-two feet below sea level. That's a dangerous road. In the days of Jesus it came to be known as the "Bloody Pass." And you know, it's possible that the priest and the Levite looked over that man on the ground and wondered if the robbers were still around. Or it's possible that they felt that the man on the ground was merely faking. And he was acting like he had been robbed and hurt, in order to seize them over there, lure them there for quick and easy seizure. And so the first question that the priest asked, the first question that the Levite asked was, "If I stop to help this man, what will happen to me?" But then the Good Samaritan came by, and he reversed the question: "If I do not stop to help this man, what will happen to him?"[3]

King's formulation is excellent. The Good Samaritan reversed the human inclination to protect ourselves and to play it safe. He was more concerned about the welfare of the stranger than about his own, and this is why the story is timeless and so powerful. The Good Samaritan overcame his fear to serve others.

He also overcame the prejudices of his day, and quite possibly his own prejudices, because the Jews and Samaritans hated each other and had for centuries. The feud ran deep, which amplifies the power of the Good Samaritan's story, because the priest and Levite who passed by the man on the side of the road were both Jewish, and the man they passed by was himself Jewish. The Good Samaritan, who was not Jewish, cast aside his prejudice and bigotry and provided care not just to a stranger, but to a man he assumed was his enemy.

In this story, Jesus was expanding the definition of what constituted a neighbor even further than we discovered on first examination. We learn what it truly means to love your neighbor as yourself: to love your enemies, too.

Notice what did *not* happen in this story. The Good Samaritan did *not* leave the man on the side of the road and return to town to report the injury to the local version of the police or medics of the day. He did *not* call on any local governing body to take care of the injured man, and he did *not* ask someone to do it for him. He acted quickly, with his own money and time.

That's the real heart of this story; the Good Samaritan *voluntarily* helped this needy person he had never met. He did it out of compassion and love for the man. Nowhere in the story do we get the sense that he acted because he felt guilty about the man on the side of the road, or that he owed the man on the side of the road something.

The Good Samaritan didn't ask anyone else to pay for the needy man's accommodations, which he could have easily done. He could easily have told the innkeeper all about what had happened and guilted him into covering the night's stay. Instead, he chose to pay for the night's stay. And he went one step further in his spontaneous act of generosity, asking the innkeeper to watch over the man for the next few days and agreeing to cover "any extra expenses." The Good Samaritan's heart for the needy man is what was on display, as was Mary of Bethany's for Jesus, and the widow's for the poor.

Was the Good Samaritan a wealthy man? We don't know, but it doesn't matter. He put his money where his heart was; his money was not as important as the health and welfare of the needy man in front of him.

As with all the stories before and after, this was a story of priorities. The Good Samaritan put his love of this stranger above all else, revealing his true heart. No one says it better anywhere in the Bible than the apostle Paul:

> *Each of you should give what you have decided in your heart to give, not reluctantly or under compulsion, for God loves a cheerful giver (2 Corinthians 9:7 NIV).*

This teaching—to give to and love others with all our hearts—has been the essence of Christianity for over 2,000 years. We, as followers of Jesus, must give to and care for the poor and needy among us, and do it cheerfully.

Voluntary giving from the heart is the complete opposite of the impersonal laws of the government that compel giving. Have you ever known anyone who "cheerfully" paid his taxes? We pay them obediently, but cheerfully? This is not an argument against worldly government welfare programs or against governments assisting the poor. It is to make clear what Jesus calls all of us to do: give of *our* time, money, and talents—and give them voluntarily and cheerfully.

Again, force and compulsion are not Jesus's way. Love is. Loving Him, and loving our neighbors—which includes the poor, the needy, our enemies, and the many rich people in need who don't know God—was what Jesus was all about.

Socialism, in the end, is a system of organizing a government. It has nothing to do with our individual hearts. It is not about voluntariness or cheerful giving or serving our Lord and Savior because He so loves us. Socialism is about using government force and compulsion to alleviate poverty and create equality. It is about a government official using the law and force to get a citizen to give to the government to give to the poor.

Nowhere in any of the stories do Jesus's teachings align with such a system. Nowhere.

"THE PREACHING OF ST PAUL AT EPHESUS"
BY EUSTACHE LE SUEUR, 1649

CHAPTER 3: WHAT JESUS AND THE BIBLE HAVE TO SAY ABOUT THEFT, PRIVATE PROPERTY, WORK, AND IDLENESS

The Bible has a lot to say about theft, private property, work, and idleness. There are many stories about all four subjects in the Bible, and one commandment alone is dedicated to two of them: the eighth commandment.

It's a mere four words, but four important words:

> *8: Thou shalt not steal (Exodus 20:15 KJV).*

Notice there are no asterisks around this short commandment. This admonition does not read, "Thou shalt not steal (* unless you feel like you have to)." It doesn't read, "Thou shalt not steal (* unless the other guy next door to you has more than you and doesn't really need it)." It doesn't read, "Thou shalt not steal (* unless you're positive you can spend it better than the guy who earned it)." And it most definitely doesn't say, "Thou shalt not steal (* but it's OK to hire someone else, like a politician, to steal it for you by force, and in the name of the public good)."

But where does the eighth commandment say anything about private property, you might be asking? It's simple. Those four words don't just *imply* there's such a thing, the eighth commandment *depends* upon the idea of private property. Think about it: how can someone steal something if it doesn't belong to someone else? Isn't that the very definition of theft—taking something that's not rightfully yours? The Bible not only permits the ownership of property (and businesses and items like cattle and coins and other commodities)—the eighth commandment insists on the idea of private property and private property rights. The Bible itself is replete with stories that include private property and people who buy and sell their own goods and trade their own commodities—cows, gold, and anything else people bought and sold to one another back then.

One system of government, communism, is *predicated* on the idea that the government owns all property—that private property is itself an evil. This is why Jesus was most certainly not a communist. Under that system, the central government itself violates the eighth commandment by virtue of its very charter—its very existence. Under that system, the government itself is God. Nowhere in the Bible is theft of anyone's private property—and in modern times that includes intellectual property such as ideas, software, compositions, and writing—viewed as anything but ungodly. Nowhere is theft of any kind seen as anything but what it is: a sin.

But the Bible, the magnificent word of God that it is, is not just a never-ending series of Thou-shalt-not's. The Bible also provides the antidote to theft and other vices and sins that have plagued mankind through the ages. The answer—the rebuttal to all sin, including theft—is Jesus. No one writes about this better than Paul in his Epistle to the Ephesians, and it is worth examining why he wrote what he wrote about all sin, before we examine what he had to say about theft.

"SAINT PAUL WRITING HIS EPISTLES"
BY VALENTIN DE BOULOGNE, 1618–1620

Remember that Paul was bringing the gospel of Jesus to a large city filled with unbelievers: Ephesus. It was a city rampant with sin and vice, and theft was one of them. Many stole out of sheer greed, others sheer envy, and others because they could not support themselves and felt compelled to steal or at least felt quite justified stealing. That was the audience and the context for Paul's writing. The people he was trying to reach were separated from God because they didn't know about Him.

Here is how Paul starts:

> *They are darkened in their understanding and separated from the life of God because of the ignorance that is in them due to the hardening of their hearts. Having lost all sensitivity, they have given themselves over to sensuality so as to*

indulge in every kind of impurity, and they are full of greed (Ephesians 4:18-19 NIV).

These words were not abstractions to the people of Ephesus—they were alive and real and relatable. Paul continued:

That, however, is not the way of life you learned when you heard about Christ and were taught in him in accordance with the truth that is in Jesus. You were taught, with regard to your former way of life, to put off your old self, which is being corrupted by its deceitful desires; to be made new in the attitude of your minds; and to put on the new self, created to be like God in true righteousness and holiness (Ephesians 4:20-24 NIV).

This is Paul at his best, talking about life before and after Jesus—his life before and after Jesus, our life before and after Jesus, and all of humanity's. With Jesus, we put off our old selves and adopt new attitudes and mindsets about life. We are all, once we put off our old selves, acutely aware of sin and its consequence. It doesn't mean we won't struggle with sin or continue to sin. But our old selves were not even aware of our sin, let alone ever convicted by it. Our old selves never considered repenting of our sin to a God who gave His only Son to die for *all* of our sins.

Paul then gives instructions we must all take seriously as believers, addressing not just theft, but the Christian alternative to theft.

Anyone who has been stealing must steal no longer, but must work, doing something useful with their own hands, that they may have something to share with those in need (Ephesians 4:28 NIV).

Paul presents two positive changes in this area. First, the Christian answer to the thief about stealing is straightforward: stop stealing. But there is also a positive alternative to theft, according to Paul: work and earn an honest living. Paul doesn't stop there, adding an additional positive—and spiritual—dimension to work. Paul frames our work in terms of what it allows us to do for other people—people who can't help themselves or are truly needy. Certainly our Lord takes great joy in any of us who once stole from others and is now using the fruit of his or her labor to help and love others. That's what Paul was writing about. Our hearts. Our new life in Jesus. And what happens when we, as Paul said, put off our old selves and become our new selves in Jesus.

Paul was a bit more explicit about the importance of work in other parts of the Bible.

The one who is unwilling to work shall not eat (2 Thessalonians 3:10 NIV).

Though that line may seem harsh on its face, that Scripture can only be properly understood in its fuller, more merciful context. Because Paul also warned against the sin that is the opposite of work: idleness. In his final instructions in 1 Thessalonians, he says this about both work and idleness:

Now we ask you, brothers and sisters, to acknowledge those who work hard among you, who care for you in the Lord and

"CHILDHOOD OF CHRIST"
BY GERARD VAN HONTHORST, 1620

who admonish you. Hold them in the highest regard in love because of their work. Live in peace with each other. And we urge you, brothers and sisters, warn those who are idle and disruptive, encourage the disheartened, help the weak, be patient with everyone (1 Thessalonians 5:12-14 NIV).

Paul also talks about the perils and dangers of idleness and idle people.

In the name of the Lord Jesus Christ, we command you, brothers and sisters, to keep away from every believer who is idle and disruptive and does not live according to the teaching you received from us. For you yourselves know how you ought to follow our example. We were not idle when we were with you, nor did we eat anyone's food without paying for it. On the contrary, we worked night and day, laboring and toiling so that we would not be a burden to any of you. We did this, not because we do not have the right to such help, but in order to offer ourselves as a model for you to imitate. For even when we were with you, we gave you this rule: "The one who is unwilling to work shall not eat" (2 Thessalonians 3:6-10 NIV).

Paul hates idleness because God hates idleness. When we look back to the beginning of the Bible—the very beginning—we learn that God didn't just work one day when He created the earth and everything on it—he worked six straight days. When God gave Moses the commandment about the Sabbath, what came before it was the command to work hard.

Six days you shall labor and do all your work, but the seventh day is a sabbath to the Lord your God. On it you shall not do any work, neither you, nor your son or daughter, nor your male or female servant, nor your animals, nor any foreigner residing in your towns (Exodus 20:8-10 NIV).

This was God's original design for mankind: we were made to work. Notice that God's design was six days of work per week—it's mankind that created the five-day work week! The truth is, work is part of what it means to be born in God's image, and God wasted no time giving out His first work assignment to mankind—a big one—to Adam.

> *The* Lord *God took the man and put him in the Garden of Eden to work it and take care of it (Genesis 2:15 NIV).*

Let's also state clearly that nowhere in the Bible does Jesus or Paul or any of the disciples have anything negative to say about people who are *unable* to work or that they are *unworthy* of our support. Indeed, it is quite the opposite. Those of us that *can* work have an obligation and duty to work so we can help those who *can't*. Not just the infirmed or the truly sick, but the youngest of our young and the oldest of our old who simply can't work, and who depend on those of us who can work to support them.

Again, this is a matter of the heart. All of us know someone—and may even have a family member—who's chosen idleness as their lifestyle. This is, in very profound respects, a form of stealing. People who have the capacity and opportunity to work but instead choose idleness are depriving the Kingdom of God of their God-given talents and robbing the truly needy of help that should have otherwise been directed at them. They are also robbing themselves of any true shot at happiness.

We must also note here that Jesus Himself had a job. "Isn't this the carpenter?" the people asked when He appeared in His hometown accompanied by His disciples. Jesus was a contractor—He worked with His hands. Paul was a tentmaker, and even on his mission trips, made a point of noting that he supported himself and refused financial support.

> *Remember, brothers, our labor and toil: we worked night and day, that we might not be a burden to any of you, while we proclaimed to you the gospel of God (1 Thessalonians 2:9 ESV).*

Paul wasn't finished making this point about hard work.

"ESQUISSE POUR L'ÉGLISE SAINT-LOUIS-D'ANTIN ,
SAINT JOSEPH PROTECTEUR DE L'ENFANCE DE JÉSUS"
BY GEORGES BECKER, 1874

For you, yourselves know how you ought to imitate us, because we were not idle when we were with you, nor did we eat anyone's bread without paying for it, but with toil and labor we worked night and day, that we might not be a burden to any of you (2 Thessalonians 3:7-8 ESV).

In short, the notion of a lazy Christian makes no sense and finds no sanction in the Bible. Indeed, we as God's children were born to work. Perhaps no one has spoken more eloquently about the divine nature of work than Reverend Dr. Martin Luther King, Jr. in his "Three Dimensions of a Complete Life" speech in Chicago on April 9, 1967, a year almost to the day before he was assassinated.

Now the thing about the length of life: after accepting ourselves and our tools, we must discover what we are called to do. And once we discover it we should set out to do it with all of the strength and all of the power that we have in our systems. And after we've discovered what God called us to do, after we've discovered our life's work, we should set out to do that work so well that the living, the dead, or the unborn couldn't do it any better.[4]

King was just getting started:

What I'm saying to you this morning, my friends, even if it falls your lot to be a street sweeper, go on out and sweep streets like Michelangelo painted pictures; sweep streets like Handel and Beethoven composed music; sweep streets like Shakespeare wrote poetry; sweep streets so well that all the hosts of heaven and earth will have to pause and say, "Here lived a great street sweeper who swept his job well."[5]

JESUS'S PARABLE OF THE TENANTS

Perhaps there is no story in the Bible less written about and more profound about stealing and property than Jesus's Parable of the Tenants.

It appears three times in the New Testament: in Mark 12, Matthew 21, and Luke 20. The story occurs right after Jesus turned over the tables in the temple courts and drove out the money and commodity traders. As noted earlier, Jesus's wrath was inspired not by the trading

"CHRIST DRIVING THE MONEY-CHANGERS FROM THE TEMPLE" BY QUINTEN MASSIJS, 16TH CENTURY

itself, but where and when the trading was taking place. He was disgusted at the abuse of God's house of prayer. Not once in the Bible does He condemn the trading of goods or animals or money in the proper place and time. He never enters a bank with a whip made of cords and ridicules money traders, nor does He enter fields or barns to express His wrath at the trading of farm animals, wheat, or corn.

After turning over the money tables and scattering the sheep and cattle, Jesus addresses the crowd, which includes some of His followers but also some Pharisees. His followers were probably not quite certain what had just happened, but the chief priests and teachers of the law were furious. Jesus was disregarding and disrespecting their traditions, as He had done a short time earlier when He healed a sick man on the Sabbath.

The chief priests and the elders challenged Jesus with two questions:

> *"By what authority are you doing these things?" they asked "And who gave you authority to do this?" (Mark 11:28 NIV).*

These were not sincere questions, of course. They were trick questions, designed to discredit Jesus, who had spent the majority of His three-year ministry performing miracles and demonstrating through signs and wonders of all kinds the source of His authority—God. But the religious establishment of the day didn't want to know or admit the truth.

That's when Jesus descends into the Parable of the Tenants:

> *"There was a landowner who planted a vineyard. He put a wall around it, dug a winepress in it and built a watchtower. Then he rented the vineyard to some farmers and moved to another place. When the harvest time approached, he sent his servants to the tenants to collect his fruit." (Matthew 21:33-34 NIV).*

To give some context, it was quite ordinary in those times for wealthy investors to buy farm property or vineyards and leave it to the care of tenant farmers, who would work the land. At harvest time, the owners would send someone to collect their portion of the harvest, with an agreed-upon amount left over for the tenant farmers to keep for their efforts.

But that's not what happened in Jesus's story.

> *"The tenants seized his servants; they beat one, killed another, and stoned a third. Then he sent other servants to*

them, more than the first time, and the tenants treated them the same way. Last of all, he sent his son to them. 'They will respect my son,' he said.

But when the tenants saw the son, they said to each other, 'This is the heir. Come, let's kill him and take his inheritance.' So they took him and threw him out of the vineyard and killed him.

"Therefore, when the owner of the vineyard comes, what will he do to those tenants?"

"He will bring those wretches to a wretched end," they replied, "and he will rent the vineyard to other tenants, who will give him his share of the crop at harvest time.'"

Jesus said to them, "Have you never read in the Scriptures: 'The stone the builders rejected has become the cornerstone; the Lord has done this, and it is marvelous in our eyes?'

"Therefore I tell you that the kingdom of God will be taken away from you and given to a people who will produce its fruit. Anyone who falls on this stone will be broken to pieces; anyone on whom it falls will be crushed."

When the chief priests and the Pharisees heard Jesus' parables, they knew he was talking about them. They looked for a way to arrest him, but they were afraid of the crowd because the people held that he was a prophet (Matthew 21:35-46 NIV).

What a remarkable, rich, and powerful story Jesus tells. At face value, it is clear who the bad guys are here, and it is not the wealthy landowners. It's the wicked tenants who steal the land that's not rightfully theirs through the act of murder. This is a violation of another of the Ten Commandments.

“PARABLE OF THE WICKED HUSBANDMEN”
BY MARTEN VAN VALCKENBORCHEDEN, 1580–1590

“ABRAHAM AND ISAAC”
BY TITIAN, 1542–1544

This parable also operates on a symbolic level. The landowner is clearly God, the vineyard obviously represents Israel, and the tenants are the religious Jewish leadership. And as the parable noted, the Jewish leaders knew Jesus was talking not just *to* them, but *about* them. They understood His words, but did not respond with humility, let alone repentance.

Their response to Jesus's parable was to instead look for a way to arrest Him. They were not at all concerned with the truth of His story, let alone with pleasing God. They were more concerned with how their actions would be perceived by the crowds who supported Jesus.

Jesus was warning those gathered around Him that the vineyard would be taken from those who rejected God's authority and granted to those that respected it. Moreover, the broader meaning here is that God's vineyard—God's bounty and abundance—was open to the Gentiles. It was open to anyone and everyone who believed in and submitted to Jesus.

What is mankind's is mankind's, but what is His is His.

A FINAL NOTE ABOUT WORK AND FAITH

There is one last thing that must be emphasized about work: it's a fundamental part of life, and one way we honor God. But our work alone doesn't—and can't—earn us our eternal salvation. The notion that we can work our way to heaven—that we can "earn" our salvation—is not true. Our salvation is God's gift to us. The apostle Paul wrote about this very thing, the difference between work and gifts.

> *Now to the one who works, wages are not credited as a gift but as an obligation (Romans 4:4 NIV).*

Think about Paul's words and relate it to your own life. If you make an agreement to pay someone $1,000 to paint your house, when they finish their work and you pay them, you can't make the claim that what you gave them was a gift, because it wasn't. The painter worked for it. He earned it. You are simply paying the painter the wages for which he worked. The wages to which you agreed.

If on that same day, you decide to give a neighbor in desperate need of transportation the title to your car out of the goodness of your heart, that would not be wages you were giving your neighbor, but a gift. A gift based on your own generosity. On your own heart. On your love for your neighbor.

You would, of course, want nothing in return, because it is a gift and you gave it for all the right reasons. You also don't want the person to whom you gave the gift feel like they owe you anything—because they don't. It is why the Bible loves not only the cheerful giver, but the secret giver.

Paul's teaching on wages, work, and faith was just one part of his lesson on salvation—the other part of his teaching, the more important part, had to do with works, faith, and salvation.

Paul chose the character of Abraham to illustrate his point. If there is one man in the Bible who *could* have inherited his eternal salvation through his works and effort, it most certainly would have been Abraham. God told Abraham to leave his land at the ripe age of 75 and Abraham obeyed. When he was asked by God to sacrifice his son Isaac, Abraham travels to Mount Moriah with his son and servants to do it. There are few characters in the Bible with a better résumé of works and good deeds.

So why did Paul write about this great Old Testament character in Romans? It was to make the precise point that even a man with a list of good deeds and accomplishments like Abraham does not earn his way to salvation.

> *What then shall we say that Abraham, our forefather according to the flesh, discovered in this matter? If, in fact, Abraham was justified by works, he had something to boast about—but not before God. What does Scripture say? "Abraham believed God, and it was credited to him as righteousness" (Romans 4:1-3 NIV).*

And there it is, three simple words that say everything: "Abraham believed God." His belief in God was the source of his salvation. It is our belief in God, too, that is the source of our salvation. No amount of effort, no amount of good works or good deeds can get us there.

Salvation is God's gift to us. If a man as great as Abraham couldn't earn his way to salvation, then there's no hope we'll earn our way to salvation, either.

"ADAM AND EVE IN THE GARDEN OF EDEN"
BY JOHANN WENZEL PETER, 1800—1829

CHAPTER 4: WHAT THE BIBLE HAS TO SAY ABOUT COVETING AND GRATITUDE

Some say that the tenth commandment is the last because it's the most insidious. It is comprised of just four words:

> *10: Thou shalt not covet (Exodus 20:17 KJV).*

Coveting, and its cousin, *envy*, drive terrible outcomes in people's lives, leading them to break multiple commandments—if not all of them. It is as destructive, if not more, than any sin, and can lead a brother to murder another brother. Coveting and envy are that bad.

Two stories about coveting and envy come to mind in the Bible: one in the Old Testament and one in the New Testament. The very first and most disturbing story about envy and coveting happens early, in Genesis: the story of Cain and Abel. It starts with some basic chronology: we learn that Cain was Adam and Eve's firstborn son, and Abel their second. We learn that it was the firstborn who got the better end of the household duties and responsibilities: he was tasked with working the soil, while his younger brother was consigned to the barn and the animals. Nowhere in the Bible does it explain why, or how Abel felt about it. But one thing we know: he didn't kill his brother over it:

> *Adam made love to his wife Eve, and she became pregnant and gave birth to Cain. She said, "With the help of the Lord I have brought forth a man." Later she gave birth to his brother Abel. Now Abel kept flocks, and Cain worked the soil (Genesis 4:1-2 NIV).*

The story pivots quickly to offerings made to God by Cain and Abel, and God's response to both:

> *In the course of time Cain brought some of the fruits of the soil as an offering to the Lord. And Abel also brought an offering—fat portions from some of the firstborn of his flock. The* LORD *looked with favor on Abel and his offering, but on Cain and his offering he did not look with favor. So Cain was very angry, and his face was downcast (Genesis 4:3-5 NIV).*

We learn in this passage that God looks at Abel's offering with pleasure, and we get a hint as to why: Abel gave generously and from the very best of his flock. We also learn that God did not look favorably upon Cain's offering—but the Bible is unclear as to why. We can assume that Cain could have done better in God's view. What happened next is most revealing not just about God's nature, but Cain's, too.

> *Then the* LORD *said to Cain, "Why are you angry? Why is your face downcast? If you do what is right, will you not be*

"ADAM AND EVE WITH CAIN AND ABEL"
BY FRA BARTOLOMEO, 1512

accepted? But if you do not do what is right, sin is crouching at your door; it desires to have you, but you must rule over it" (Genesis 4:6-7 NIV).

God shows His loving and merciful side to Cain. He sees that Cain is dejected and angry with what he perceives is an unjust and unfair verdict, and gives Cain some advice. He also encourages Cain to do what is right when the next offering comes, but also cautions Cain that if he doesn't, sin is "crouching at his door." The sin of coveting, comparison, and envy, God explained to Cain, is like a predator waiting to devour you.

"CAIN LEADETH ABEL TO DEATH"
BY JAMES TISSOT, 1896–1902

Rather than take God's advice, Cain allows his bitterness and envy to get the best of him, and launches a premeditated, duplicitous plot to murder his own brother.

> *Now Cain said to his brother Abel, "Let's go out to the field." While they were in the field, Cain attacked his brother Abel and killed him (Genesis 4:8 NIV).*

We learn from the story that before Cain was angry at Abel, he was first angry at God. This is precisely how envy weaves its destructive path: it rarely starts with the *object* of our envy. It starts with the perceived *source* of injustice and unfairness: God. It starts with a human being looking up and crying out in anger, "Why not me, God? Why have you not favored me? Why have you not given me what you gave someone else?"

God's perceived unfairness is the source of Cain's rage. Abel, it turns out, is a mere object of his envy and rage. Abel is the unsuspecting and innocent victim in a drama played out between Cain and God. He's guilty of nothing more than doing and being good, and being in the wrong place at the wrong time.

This is the power and danger of envy. It's a sin that can strike at any time, and when we least expect it. It can happen when we see a new car in our neighbor's driveway. It can happen when a friend gets a big promotion, or a family member gets a big raise. It can happen to any of us, at any time, and for any reason.

Novelist Gore Vidal once said:

> *Every time a friend succeeds, I die a little.*[6]

It would be easy to dismiss Vidal as a bad guy and bad friend, but we know, if we dared to admit it, what he's talking about. It is indeed one of Satan's great weapons that he uses to separate us from God and pit human against human. And once it goes to work, envy is all consuming. It grips the heart, occupies the mind and relentlessly craves more of our emotions, more of our time, and more of our effort.

Once unleashed, envy and covetousness can never be satisfied: that craving for something someone else has or treasures is unquenchable, and always, we will find someone else who has something we wish we had. Life's injustices act as the fuel to envy, and life's unfair outcomes act as the match that ignites the flame, all while Satan stands alongside us, egging us on.

And that's why coveting and envy are so dangerous: the love of God is turned on its head and instead becomes hatred of our neighbors, friends, and family. Where we should be inclined to celebrate the success of our loved ones, envy turns a basic good into an unmitigated evil.

One passage in the Bible gets at this idea very plainly:

> *What causes fights and quarrels among you? Don't they come from your desires that battle within you? You desire but do not have, so you kill. You covet but you cannot get what you want, so you quarrel and fight. You do not have because you do not ask God. When you ask, you do not receive, because you ask with wrong motives, that you may spend what you get on your pleasures (James 4:1-4 NIV).*

There it is, plain and simple:

> *You desire what you do not have, so you kill.*

And notice that the Lord knows our motives and our intentions when we ask things of Him, and when we pray to Him. God knows our minds. God cares about our minds. We run into this idea again and again in the Bible—He knows our minds. And He knows our hearts, too. And He cares about both.

THE PRODIGAL SON, AND HIS LOST BROTHER

There is one additional story worth telling about envy and coveting. While not as dramatic or tragic, it is equally disturbing: The Prodigal Older Brother. I know what you're thinking. Where is *that* story in the Bible? I know the Prodigal Son story, but the Prodigal Brother?

Let's review, because this story is about so many things, especially God's character. God is always with us, and He will always welcome us back if we've strayed. Always.

The parable begins with a man and his two sons, the younger of whom asks his father for his share of the family's estate. The younger son is impatient. He doesn't want to wait for his father's death to enjoy his portion of the inheritance. He wants it now. The father, without protest, grants his younger son's request and his son soon liquidates his father's portion of his estate.

We know what happens next, and we know the story well because we've seen stories like it in our own lives. The young son travels to a distant country where he lives wildly and recklessly, quickly squandering all of his money. To make matters worse, the country he ran to experiences a famine, and in a desperate attempt to survive, he takes a job feeding pigs. He's so hungry he even desires to eat the pig's food.

We all know what happens next to the younger son in this, one of Jesus's greatest parables.

> *"When he came to his senses, he said, 'How many of my father's hired servants have food to spare, and here I am starving to death! I will set out and go back to my father and say to him: Father, I have sinned against heaven and against you. I am no longer worthy to be called your son; make me like one of your hired servants.' So he got up and went to his father." (Luke 15:17-20a NIV).*

What happens next may be the best example of what living a Christlike life looks like. Before he's even aware of his younger son's repentant heart, the father doesn't just wait to greet his son—he *runs* to him. Filled with compassion, he runs to his younger son with a joyous rather than a hard heart, showering his son with gifts—and love.

The final part of this story may be the most compelling: the reaction of the *older* brother to his father's joy. Because Jesus wasn't just telling us this story to remind us of what a Christian father's love—and His love—looks like. He also wanted to paint a picture of what envy looks like, too. How envy steals joy and thwarts not only a father's love, but God's:

> *"Meanwhile, the older son was in the field. When he came near the house, he heard music and dancing. So he called one of the servants and asked him what was going on. 'Your brother has come,' he replied, 'and your father has killed the fattened calf because he has him back safe and sound.'*
>
> *"The older brother became angry and refused to go in. So his father went out and pleaded with him. But he answered his father, 'Look! All these years I've been slaving for you and never disobeyed your orders. Yet you never gave me even a young*

“THE PRODIGAL SON FEEDING SWINE”
BY BARTOLOMÉ ESTEBAN MURILLO, 1660s

"THE RETURN OF THE PRODIGAL SON"
BY ANONYMOUS, 1630

> *goat so I could celebrate with my friends. But when this son of yours who has squandered your property with prostitutes comes home, you kill the fattened calf for him!'"* (Luke 15:23-30 NIV).

There it is: the older son, Jesus notes, is unhappy not with his *brother* but his *father*. Angry at what he sensed is unjust and unfair. This is what envy, covetousness, and comparison create. It shifts the focus from God to self, and from selflessness to selfishness. There was not a single ounce of joy expressed by the older brother that his younger brother had returned home in one piece and with a repentant heart. He did not express a single ounce of happiness for his father, either. The older son was too absorbed with his own feelings and his sense of unfairness at what he saw as an unjust gift from his father to his younger brother.

One sentence, the words of the older brother to the father, says it all:

> *"'You never gave me even a young goat so I could celebrate with my friends'" (Luke 15:29 NIV).*

Jesus tells this story because it shows how envy and comparison can devolve into self-righteousness, heartlessness, and a total separation from our earthly father's love and our heavenly father's love.

The father then addresses his older son's envy and the anger that sprang from it with understanding and compassion:

> *"'My son,' the father said, 'you are always with me, and everything I have is yours. But we had to celebrate and be glad, because this brother of yours was dead and is alive again; he was lost and is found'" (Luke 15:31-32 NIV).*

What we learn from this story is that there was not just one lost son, but two sons separated from God. By the end of this story, and despite having lived close to his father for all of those years and honoring his father, the older brother is further from his father's love—and God's—than the repentant younger brother.

What is the answer to coveting and envy in the Bible? That, too, is simple: gratitude for all that God has given us and blessed us with, no matter our circumstance. The apostle Paul makes the case.

"ENVY (INVIDIA) FROM THE SEVEN DEADLY SINS"
BY PIETER VAN DER HEYDEN, PIETER BRUEGHEL THE ELDER,
AND HIERONYMUS COCK; 1558

> *Rejoice always, pray continually, give thanks in all circumstances; for this is God's will for you in Christ Jesus (1 Thessalonians 5:16-18 NIV).*

There will always be people around us with more or less than us: wealth, health, tragedy, happiness, and time. Our work as Christians is to love our neighbors—and not just the ones we perceive as worse or better off. A family with great wealth may be suffering from bad health, and a family with great health and happiness may be on the brink of financial ruin.

Gratitude saves us from the treacherous shores of envy and discontent, and it is impossible to be at peace with our circumstance without gratitude. It is easy for envy and coveting to sneak into our hearts, and steal our joy, and steal our relationship with God.

In struggle and hardship, it is easy to get angry with God and focus on what He has not done for us and has done for others. The Bible gives us clear instructions:

> *Consider it pure joy, my brothers and sisters, whenever you face trials of many kinds, because you know that the testing of your faith produces perseverance (James 1:2-3 NIV).*

It's important to feel grateful *during* hardships, the Bible instructs us. It is also important to feel grateful *for* your hardships. In our lives, we can all look back at our worst travails and hardships and see that it was an opportunity to lean on God, to learn from God, and to get closer to God. And always, God is there for us, in our best times and our worst. It is easy for us to forget God during our good times. Gratitude is God's rebuttal—God's antidote—to envy, coveting, and resentment.

Our hearts and minds must remain on guard against envy, covetousness, and anger. What could Cain have done differently? What could the older brother have done differently in the Parable of the Prodigal Son? What matters isn't what they chose to do, but what we choose to do when we get angry at God with some result or circumstance in life we believe is unfair or unjust.

At some point or another, we may be any of the characters in those stories. Jesus told those stories not for His benefit, but ours. When we begin to be consumed with anger at God, or envy toward a family member, friend, or neighbor, we can ask ourselves a simple question: Do we want to be the older brother who welcomes back home his lost younger brother, or not?

If we are parents, will we run to our long-lost son or daughter who went astray, or lecture the returning child about the error of their ways? We get to choose. Always, God lets us choose: Satan's way or His way.

It is said in sports and war that the best defense is a good offense. It is true with spiritual warfare, too, and we must see clearly that envy and covetousness are not of Jesus, but of Satan. Gratitude is a weapon designed by God not just to protect our hearts and minds from sin, but inoculate them and chase those sins away.

Those two stories from the Bible make it clear how easy it is to turn from God and allow ourselves to be filled with bitterness and consumed with envy. The answer, always, is to turn to God seeking His understanding, comfort, mercy, and trust. Always, turning back to God is the best choice.

Every time we compare our lives to others around us, every time we feel bitterness start to build and envy start to rule our hearts, and every time someone around us—politicians especially—try to tap our sense of envy and coveting by stoking the fire of life's inequalities and

"CHRIST IN GETHSEMANE"
BY HEINRICH HOFMANN, 1886

unfairness, we have a choice to make: choose to run with the sin and separate from God, or get closer to Him by choosing gratitude instead.

When envy and coveting come knocking at our door, we can choose the Enemy, or choose God. We can shake our fist at God and wreak havoc on the lives around us, or humbly get on our knees in gratitude to the God who so loved the world, He sent His only Son to the earth to die for our sins.

Jesus Himself reminds all of us about this when he's asked by one of His disciples:

> *"Lord, teach us to pray" (Luke 11:1 NIV).*

Jesus's short answer to the request can be found in the Gospel According to Luke. The longer version, part of Jesus's Sermon on the Mount, can be found in the Gospel According to Matthew.

> *"This, then, is how you should pray:*
>
> *'Our Father in heaven,*
> *hallowed be your name,*
> *your kingdom come,*
> *your will be done,*
> *on earth as it is in heaven.*
> *Give us today our daily bread.*
> *And forgive us our debts,*
> *as we also have forgiven our debtors.*
> *And lead us not into temptation,*
> *but deliver us from the evil one'"*
> *(Matthew 6:9-13 NIV).*

This prayer is so powerful for so many reasons, first and foremost because it is the prayer Jesus tells us to pray. It orients us in all the right ways, always focused on Him and the way He provides for us. And what He requires of us, especially as it relates to how we should treat our neighbors—with compassion and mercy—as He treats us. Only He can deliver us from Satan. Only Jesus can save us from envy and covetousness. Jesus is never the source of envy and covetousness: He is the solution.

What is even more powerful than the Lord's Prayer are Jesus's prayer instructions: instructions about *how* to pray, not just *what* to pray.

> *"But when you pray, go into your room, close the door and pray to your Father, who is unseen. Then your Father, who sees what is done in secret, will reward you. And when you pray, do not keep on babbling like pagans, for they think they will be heard because of their many words. Do not be like them, for your Father knows what you need before you ask him" (Matthew 6:6-8 NIV).*

And there it is once again: Jesus is most concerned about our minds and hearts. He wants us praying, and praying for the right reasons. Jesus knows those are Satan's entry points, and Jesus warns us, again and again, that without him, we have no chance.

And that with him, we can all be delivered from the evil one.

“CHRIST AND THE GOOD THIEF”
BY TITIAN, 1566

CHAPTER 5: BACK TO THE BEGINNING: IS JESUS A SOCIALIST?

We've covered a lot of ground. We've covered wealth and money, and the fact that Jesus doesn't hate either. It's the love of money He has a problem with. We've covered proper stewardship of God's resources and money—and bad stewardship, as explained by Jesus in the Parable of the Tenants. We've covered voluntary giving—generous and cheerful giving, the kind Jesus loves—and coercive giving through the force of government, about which Jesus has very little to say except that we must pay it. We've covered work, which the Bible values, and idleness, which the Bible doesn't. We've covered property rights, which the Bible values, and theft, which God deplores. And last, we've covered envy and coveting, and God's antidote to both: gratitude.

So, we end things where we began, with a question: Is Jesus a socialist? Let's return to the definition of socialism from *Dictionary.com*:

> *Noun: a theory or system of social organization that advocates the ownership and control of the means of production and*

> *distribution, capital, land, etc., by the community as a whole, usually through a centralized government.*[7]

In short, socialism calls for no private ownership of anything. Not a private business, not a car, not a home, not even an idea. It's not yours, God's, or God's gift to mankind—the state owns everything. A centralized government—a centralized authority—controls everything. The all-powerful state runs our lives under socialism and communism and uses its coercive power—force of law—to achieve its aims.

We know that such a world is not a biblical one, because we know the Bible values private property and hates theft. And we know that under socialist and communist regimes throughout history, it's the government itself that has been the very worst thief. Throughout history, government officials have used the promise of doing good as a pretext for theft. They claim to want to transfer wealth from the rich to the poor, but invariably make everyone poor—and keep the wealth they've appropriated through force for themselves and for their own personal power. The result for the citizen? Everyone is equal because everyone is now poor.

Look no further than the story of Jesus and Mary and the perfume, as we did earlier in this series, to understand how thieves can masquerade as humanitarian do-gooders. What was Judas's intent when he rebuked Mary for pouring her expensive perfume on Jesus's feet?

> *He did not say this because he cared about the poor but because he was a thief; as keeper of the money bag, he used to help himself to what was put into it (John 12:6 NIV).*

Anyone who has spent any time in this world knows that there are—and always have been—politicians who claim to *publicly* care about the poor, but who *privately* care about their own wealth and power. They steal from good people who could have put their own money to better use serving the poor, thus depriving the poor—and the body of Christ—of sincere and voluntary acts of compassion and love.

And remember Jesus's reply to Judas?

> *"Leave her alone," Jesus replied. "It was intended that she should save this perfume for the day of my burial. You will always have the poor among you, but you will not always have me" (John 12:7-8 NIV).*

It was a blistering attack against Judas because Jesus knew Judas's heart. There was no love in Judas's heart when he rebuked Mary. And there is no heart or love in socialism. It is all earthly goals—political, economic, and social goals with the state as goal-setter and enforcer, replacing God as the central authority in the life of its citizens.

That's the problem with socialism. Its aims seem good and decent with what appear to be worthy goals. The list is almost always the same: eliminate inequality, eliminate poverty, eliminate hunger, and provide free health care, housing, and transportation. But there's a fatal flaw; believers in socialism assume that the people administering their idealized state are worthy of the task. That is perhaps the greatest—and most fundamental flaw—with socialism. It does not consider the Christian reality that we live in a fallen world, filled with fallen people. The world is filled with inequities that Jesus Himself didn't try to fix or cure while He was here, though He could have if He desired.

Why, we must ask ourselves as Christians, should mankind try to solve through government power and coercion what Jesus was trying to solve through the transformation of individual minds and hearts?

It is worth noting here that there is nothing wrong with governments raising taxes to try to help the poor, and Jesus made no claim to the contrary. What is deeply troubling—and what cuts against the teachings of Jesus—is a state that becomes so powerful and rapacious that it leaves little if any room for Christian charity and Christian love, let alone private property, as well as proper incentives that reward work and punish idleness.

That's the problem with socialism and communism. Both crowd out God's love, as well as the ordinary Jesus follower's ability to give to the poor and help the needy. Socialism and communism also crowd out our tithe to our churches, which sustains them and allows them to serve their communities. That may be the biggest problem with communism and socialism. Jesus's followers have less to give to God because the government has gobbled it all up.

THE RADICAL MESSAGE OF JESUS

The radical message of Jesus is not the elimination of hunger or misery or misfortune in our time. It's the call for each of us to love and help the hungry, the miserable, and the unfortunate. When the state takes up the work for helping the poor that Jesus left for us to do, there are tragic consequences. It deprives the recipients of the opportunity to experience Jesus through that act of *voluntary* and *personal* compassion, as well as the gratitude that can flow from that act of Christlike love and compassion.

Those state benefits—that state charity—create the opposite effect on the recipient; the experience of gratitude from a voluntary and personal act of Christian love is now replaced with the sense of entitlement felt from an involuntary and impersonal act of the state. The desires of Jesus are turned upside down.

Lest we forget, not one of us thinks of the word *love* when we pay our taxes, or more accurately, when our taxes get removed from our checks every other week. That's what we get in the end with socialism: givers without love and recipients without gratitude.

There are other problems with socialism and communism—especially the promise of a world with equal outcomes and a world without financial or economic worry. Does God really desire for us to have all our material and physical needs met by our government? To have a free and easy life without responsibilities to and for each other? And without God's help?

The Bible speaks to these questions often and consistently. And always, the answer is this: God will provide! Let's turn to Scripture for some examples:

> *And my God will supply every need of yours according to his riches in glory in Christ Jesus (Philippians 4:19 ESV).*
>
> *"Therefore do not be anxious, saying, 'What shall we eat?' or 'What shall we drink?' or 'What shall we wear?' For the Gentiles seek after all these things, and your heavenly Father knows that you need them all" (Matthew 6:31-32 ESV).*
>
> *"If you then, who are evil, know how to give good gifts to your children, how much more will your Father who is in heaven give good things to those who ask him!" (Matthew 7:11 ESV).*
>
> *"Consider the ravens: they neither sow nor reap, they have neither storehouse nor barn, and yet God feeds them. Of how much more value are you than the birds!" (Luke 12:24 ESV).*

“THE TEMPTATION OF CHRIST BY THE DEVIL”
BY FÉLIX JOSEPH BARRIAS, 1860

One thing we know for sure: Jesus promises us He will provide for us, but He never promises us a risk-free or tragedy-free life, nor material wealth. And Jesus never forces us to do anything. He doesn't force us to love Him or follow Him. He loves us enough to allow us to make that choice for ourselves. We must willingly volunteer to become a Christian, because coercion was not a part of Jesus's teaching—love was the animating force of His ministry.

Jesus didn't have much to say about government, and often challenged government officials for their arrogance and abuse of power. All Jesus had to say about government was a simple line:

> *"Render to Caesar the things that are Caesar's, and to God the things that are God's" (Mark 12:17; Matthew 22:21 ESV).*

This was Jesus's way of drawing a distinction between two kingdoms: one ephemeral and one eternal. Make sure you give to Caesar his due—the temporary things of the material world—and to God what is God's, Jesus was saying. And God always comes first. Beyond that, He had little to say. It wasn't exactly a ringing endorsement for socialism!

One thing that bears repeating from earlier is this; if Jesus had wanted to rule the earth and become an earthly King, He could have, but He didn't desire power. In Satan's final temptation, he took Jesus to a high mountain and made Jesus an offer most mortals would have accepted.

> *And he said to him, "All these I will give you, if you will fall down and worship me" (Matthew 4:9 ESV).*

But Jesus was not impressed by the offer.

"Be gone, Satan! For it is written, 'You shall worship the Lord your God and him only'" (Matthew 4:10 ESV).

Clearly, Jesus did not visit us to manage our earthly political affairs or to create the best form of government—that was not His interest. His mission field was us. Jesus's mission field was our minds, hearts, and eternal souls. His ministry was a deeply personal one, not a political one.

Jesus didn't preach a "chicken in every pot" when He walked here on earth. If He wanted to end poverty in His time, He could have done that. He was, after all, Jesus! But during His three-year ministry, He spent little time feeding the hungry—only a few times, most memorably at the mountain on the other side of the Sea of Galilee. But as we indicated earlier, that story was less about feeding the hungry masses than letting them see for themselves who He was and witness with their own eyes the miracles He could perform through and with His disciples.

When the people saw the sign that he had done, they said, "This is indeed the Prophet who is to come into the world!" (John 6:14 ESV).

As for wealth redistribution, Jesus never mentioned it or even hinted at it in the Bible. In one instance He was asked to play the role of equity judge and settle an outstanding claim over an inheritance, but Jesus quickly refused.

Someone in the crowd said to him, "Teacher, tell my brother to divide the family inheritance with me."

Jesus replied, "Man, who appointed me a judge or an arbiter between you?" Then he said to them, "Watch out! Be on your

“ALL THINGS DIE, BUT ALL WILL BE RESURRECTED THROUGH GOD’S LOVE”
BY LEON FRÉDÉRIC, 1893–1918

guard against all kinds of greed; life does not consist in an abundance of possessions" (Luke 12:13-15 NIV).

Jesus did not suggest massive wealth redistribution on a scale socialists and communists dream about. Socialists don't want equality of opportunity, but equality of outcome. Force is always the path to get there.

Jesus cared about our *hearts* when it came to our money, our talents, and our gifts, and warned us about the perils of comparing ourselves to others. Jesus warned us about comparing our lot in life with a brother's or a neighbor's. He warned us about and told stories about the dangers of coveting and comparison and envy. This is why it seems so odd to caricature Jesus, our Lord and Savior, as the embodiment of a man-made political system like socialism. Jesus was not concerned about differences in material outcomes. It's the point—among many—of the Parable of the Talents. Each of the men was given varying amounts of money to manage, but God wasn't concerned with what the men *started* with. He was much more concerned with their stewardship of that with which they were entrusted. He was much more concerned with the hearts of each of those three men.

That's the thing about socialists: they're obsessed with material outcomes and with economic inequalities which they see as their mission to end here on earth. Jesus cares much more about heart and spiritual outcomes. The outcome that matters most to Jesus is each of our eternal outcomes.

SCARCITY VS. ABUNDANCE

The biggest problem with socialists and communists as it relates to the Bible is abundance. Socialists and communists don't believe in God's *abundance*. They don't believe that God created the heavens and the earth, the trees and the animals, the oceans and the stars. Because if they did, they would know that our God is an abundant God.

Socialists and communists instead see *scarcity* everywhere they turn. It's why they so desire to redistribute wealth—because they have no idea what the source of all the wealth in the world truly is—material, spiritual, and otherwise: God Himself. Socialists see the world and wealth as static and they try their best to control that wealth, to put limits on that wealth, and to demonize that wealth. They don't see God as abundant and loving.

In short, the socialist mindset can best be described as a scarcity mindset. The world in their eyes is finite, and thus, they must concoct government rules and regulations to control the existing wealth we have on earth and redistribute it to create equality of outcomes.

God's mindset is the opposite; it is one of infinite abundance. Jesus Himself explains in the Parable of the Mustard Seed and the Yeast how abundance works:

> *Then Jesus asked, "What is the kingdom of God like? What shall I compare it to? It is like a mustard seed, which a man took and planted in his garden. It grew and became a tree, and the birds perched in its branches."*
>
> *Again he asked, "What shall I compare the kingdom of God to? It is like yeast that a woman took and mixed into about sixty pounds of flour until it worked all through the dough" (Luke 13:18-21 NIV).*

Jesus is talking metaphorically in this story about how we can enter the Kingdom of Heaven, but He is also explaining how abundance works. He explains how human ingenuity and productivity can and should work to benefit humanity.

There's nothing miraculous about yeast or flour. God designed them both. But He also designed us to be creative enough to combine them. And He also designed us to do the work—and hone the skills—to turn flour and yeast into bread.

Anyone who has ever turned yeast and flour into bread knows one thing: it's hard work. It requires diligence, skill, and patience to turn those seemingly unrelated ingredients into bread—something that is valued highly in the marketplace and in households and restaurants everywhere.

Turning yeast and flour into bread is not for the fainthearted. The smallest variances in weather, humidity, and the water can change outcomes. It takes a real commitment—real heart—to do the job well day after day.

If anything, this parable and others point to a system of life—free markets—that is more in alignment with the values of Jesus than socialism or communism. The key word in *free markets* is the word *free*. Not free as in no cost, but free as in *freedom*. God has a lot to say about freedom in the Bible. Jesus told even more parables along these lines. The Parable of the Sower, the Parable of the Weeds, and the Parable of the Mustard Seed all deal with provision, abundance, and stewardship, as well as life, not just here on earth, but also in the Kingdom of Heaven.

Let's look at the Parable of the Sower (sometimes called the Parable of the Soils). It's worth reading because it combines profound worldly and eternal instruction.

It starts with Jesus sitting by a lake, with crowds gathered around Him so large, He got on a *boat* to share this story. Here's how it started and ended:

"PARABLE OF THE SOWER"
BY PIETER BRUEGHEL THE ELDER, 1557

Then he told them many things in parables, saying: "A farmer went out to sow his seed. As he was scattering the seed, some fell along the path, and the birds came and ate it up. Some fell on rocky places, where it did not have much soil. It sprang up quickly, because the soil was shallow. But when the sun came up, the plants were scorched, and they withered because they had no root. Other seed fell among thorns, which grew up and choked the plants. Still other seed fell on good soil, where it produced a crop—a hundred, sixty or thirty times what was sown. Whoever has ears, let them hear.'"

The disciples came to him and asked, "Why do you speak to the people in parables?"

He replied, "Because the knowledge of the secrets of the kingdom of heaven has been given to you, but not to them. Whoever has will be given more, and they will have an abundance. Whoever does not have, even what they have will be taken from them" (Matthew 13:3-13 NIV).

The dominant metaphor in this story is simple: some ground is better able to receive seeds than others. Some ground is more fertile than others. So, too, with our hearts, Jesus explains. In this story, the soil represents us. It represents our hearts.

Again and again, we learn that Jesus cares most about our hearts. If God's word is accepted, but not cultivated, it will wither. It is only for those who truly cultivate their faith, that real bounty and abundance will be found. There is a literal nature to this story too. In the first century, agriculture was the big industry of its day. This parable depicts how farmers use their talents to make their land more receptive to growth and produce greater yields. It shows that by using their human ingenuity and creativity as well as good old-fashioned industriousness, farmers can produce bountiful crops that can help feed not only the farmer's families, but other families, too.

Properly preparing soil in both the first century and the 21st century takes great knowledge, discipline, and understanding. Like the hard work and skill it takes to turn yeast and flour into bread, it takes years of study, skill, diligence, patience, and great managerial talent to operate a farm. You don't tend to associate the words *lazy* or *idle* with the word *farmer*. God provides the soil and the seeds, but it takes human industry, innovation, and effort to turn those seeds and soil into an annual crop. The farmer that doesn't study, work, or grow deeper in his knowledge of his field, will as surely wither as the believer who doesn't know or study the word of God.

No American has written more eloquently about the subjects of cultivation, abundance, wealth-creation, and socialism than Larry Reed, president emeritus of the Foundation for Economic Education. He wrote:

> *The empirical evidence today is overwhelming that, as Montesquieu observed two centuries ago, "Countries are well cultivated, not as they are fertile, but as they are free." Nations possessing the most economic freedom (and the smallest governments) have higher rates of long-term economic growth and are more prosperous than those that engage in socialistic and redistributive practices. The countries with the lowest levels of economic freedom also have the lowest standards of living. Free countries and their people are the greatest charitable givers, whereas, on net balance, socialist ones are decisively on the receiving end. Why is this relevant? Because you can't redistribute anything to anybody if it's not created by somebody in the first place, and the evidence strongly suggests that the only lasting thing that socialist and redistributive arrangements do for poor people is give them lots of company.*[8]

Reed closed out his thoughts on the subject with these words:

> *In Jesus's teachings and in many other parts of the New Testament, Christians—indeed, all people—are advised to be of "generous spirit," to care for one's family, to help the*

> *poor, to assist widows and orphans, to exhibit kindness and to maintain the highest character. How all that gets translated into the dirty business of coercive, vote-buying, politically driven redistribution schemes is a problem for prevaricators with agendas. It's not a problem for scholars of what the Bible actually says and doesn't say.*[9]

We must also remember that the worst political regimes of the past century-and-a-half were committed to the ideas of socialism and communism. The word *NAZI* was shorthand for the National Socialist Workers Party, and it was Hitler's design to seize the public square and concentrate power for the so-called good of the German people. First Hitler targeted and illed the weakest in his population—the handicapped and those with mental illness or deficiencies in order to make the Aryan race stronger. Soon, it was his racism that led to the annihilation of Jews, the worst genocide in recorded history. This then led to a world war that would lead to the death of 60 million people.

Only the communist regimes run by Joseph Stalin (The Soviet Union) and Mao Zedong (founder of the People's Republic of China) were comparable to Hitler's atrocities. The two communist rulers worked their evil ways differently than the fascist dictator in Germany, but the outcome was the same: a strong, centralized, authoritarian government that caused the death of millions of their own people. This is all under the false promise of using the government to create a heaven on earth—a place free from inequality, injustice, hunger, and oppression.

None of this by any means makes Jesus a capitalist. But what drives the success of free markets and the human ingenuity and innovation it produces is the voluntary nature of the marketplace itself. It is the voluntary nature of free markets that has lifted billions of people around the world out of poverty, extended life spans with miraculous cures for diseases, and so much more. No one forces people to eat at Chick-fil-A. People have the freedom to *choose* to eat there because the company—its leadership and its 140,000[10] team members—serve great food and offer excellent value. If they stop doing that—or take their customers for granted—those customers have the freedom to choose to spend their hard-earned money elsewhere.

The wealth that this alternative to socialism and communism has unleashed around the world is undeniable because it is the opposite of

"PARABLE OF THE SOWER"
BY MARTEN VAN VALCKENBORCH, 1580–1590

socialism and communism. It depends entirely on the *voluntary* and *free* exchange of goods and services. Its voluntary nature is free market capitalism's secret sauce, unearthing the God-given talents of human beings throughout the world.

One of the great humanitarians of the 20th and 21st centuries is also the leader of one of the world's most successful rock bands: Bono, the lead singer and band leader of U2, and a Christian, too. He, an admitted man of the left, has worked for decades trying to reduce hunger and poverty and disease in the poorest places on earth. In 2022, the world-famous social activist made a confession of sorts about the error of his thinking about world-wide poverty.

> *I thought that if we just redistributed resources, then we could solve every problem. I now know that's not true. There's a funny moment when you realize that as an activist: The off-ramp out of extreme poverty is, ugh, commerce, it's entrepreneurial capitalism.*[11]

None of this means that Jesus is a capitalist. Indeed, capitalism unmoored from mercy and love of neighbor, from compassion and concern for poor and vulnerable segments of society, from government safety nets for the most vulnerable among us, is not worthy of the name Christian, either. The worth and dignity of human beings cannot be measured by outputs, gross domestic product, or income.

One story Jesus tells that certainly befuddles capitalists is the Parable of the Workers in the Vineyard. Before we dig into this remarkable story in detail, it is worth reading the entire parable in Jesus's own words:

For the kingdom of heaven is like a landowner who went out early in the morning to hire workers for his vineyard. He agreed to pay them a denarius for the day and sent them into his vineyard.

About nine in the morning he went out and saw others standing in the marketplace doing nothing. He told them, "You also go and work in my vineyard, and I will pay you whatever is right." So they went.

He went out again about noon and about three in the afternoon and did the same thing. About five in the afternoon he went out and found still others standing around. He asked them, "Why have you been standing here all day long doing nothing?"

"Because no one has hired us," they answered.

He said to them, "You also go and work in my vineyard."

When evening came, the owner of the vineyard said to his foreman, "Call the workers and pay them their wages, beginning with the last ones hired and going on to the first."

The workers who were hired about five in the afternoon came and each received a denarius. So when those came who were hired first, they expected to receive more. But each one of them also received a denarius. When they received it, they began to grumble against the landowner. "These who were hired last worked only one hour,' they said, 'and you have made them equal to us who have borne the burden of the work and the heat of the day."

But he answered one of them, "I am not being unfair to you, friend. Didn't you agree to work for a denarius? Take your pay

"THE RED VINEYARD"
BY VINCENT VAN GOGH, 1888

and go. I want to give the one who was hired last the same as I gave you. Don't I have the right to do what I want with my own money? Or are you envious because I am generous?"

So the last will be first, and the first will be last (Matthew 20:1-16).

What a story, and an uncomfortable one for capitalists. How utterly unfair that the worker who works the least gets paid the same as the worker who works the most! What kind of a businessman, let alone employer, is this landowner? What kind of incentives is this landowner advancing? Why would anyone want to show up early to work for a boss like this? The mind of a capitalist might very well be asking these questions of this story. Just what kind of lessons is this parable teaching?

The fact is, Jesus was not teaching an economics class in this lesson. Moreover, the landowner honored his promises to each and every one of the workers. When the workers started to grumble about the unfairness of landowner's pay plan, he let them have it:

"I am not being unfair to you, friend. Didn't you agree to work for a denarius? Take your pay and go" (Matthew 20:13-14).

The landowner wasn't finished, letting them know what he thought of their claims, and what he knew about their hearts.

"Don't I have the right to do what I want with my own money? Or are you envious because I am generous?" (Matthew 20:15).

The landowner knew what Jesus knows about all of us: that we are too often unhappy with God when He does something we believe is unfair, does what we believe is unjust, even as He honors His promise to us. And we know what coveting and comparison does to the human heart: they harden our hearts, separate us from our neighbors, and separate us from God.

Jesus told this story not to explain our earthly economy, but the heavenly one. Jesus doesn't care if you have been a convert for 70 years or 70 minutes. And He doesn't want us to care either. This parable is not about landowners, or wages, or equity, or fair pay and play. It is a story about God's *goodness*. It is a story about God's generosity and compassion, and a glimpse into the heavenly realm. It is about what God desires for all of us: a good heart cleansed of covetousness and envy and filled with love and gratitude.

This parable is, in the end, a story about the grace of God—and His mercy, too—especially to people who least expect it, believe they haven't earned it, and all of us who don't deserve it.

The fact is, God's justice, mercy, and love are so much bigger than the justice, mercy, and love we humans exhibit. Jesus told this story not to teach about remuneration, or how fairly wealth or health is distributed to us. He told this parable to teach us about *salvation*, which is available to all of us no matter our wealth, health, social status or past.

If capitalism has a defect, it is that too many people treat it as their God. They worship at the altar of capitalism, and the scorecard of unbridled capitalism—which is accumulated wealth.

Jesus, through this parable, lets the world know *His* scorecard is very different than the earthly scorecards we know and with which we measure success. We measure winners and losers. No single sentence Jesus utters in the Bible makes that clearer than the last one in this story:

> *"So the last will be first, and the first will be last" (Matthew 20:16).*

Jesus is most certainly not a capitalist. That is simple-minded and just plain wrong. But Jesus is most certainly not a socialist either, not by any serious study of the Scripture or of Jesus's words and deeds.

Jesus is most certainly not a Democrat or Republican, nor a man of the political left or right. He doesn't fit into any box or man-made construct or narrative. The differences that divide mankind—the earthly things that separate us—are of no interest or consequence to Him. Differences in class, ethnicity, or cultural background are man-made battlelines. The only division that matters—the only choice He cares about—is one we are all given. And always, that choice is to follow Jesus or not. The only thing that matters to Jesus is whether we choose to believe He alone is the source of our eternal salvation. That is a profound personal choice. A profound spiritual choice. A profound heart and mind choice.

Jesus was so far ahead of His time that He was the OMC: the original multiculturalist. He knows and has always known that all who accept Him and follow Him are brothers and sisters in Jesus. No matter our skin color, gender, or ethnic heritage, Jesus is our beginning and our end. Our identity is in Him and through Him.

To reduce Jesus's life, death, and resurrection—and His profound teachings—to a deeply flawed and man-made political system that uses force and coercion to help the poor is a mixture of folly and arrogance. Yet there are some people outside the Christian community (and some inside it, too) who believe that the life and teachings of Jesus supports the political and economic theory known as socialism.

To them—and for all of us who try to shrink Jesus to align with our own worldviews—this last verse from the Bible is worth keeping close.

> *"For my thoughts are not your thoughts, neither are your ways my ways," declares the Lord (Isaiah 55:8-9 NIV).*

Endnotes

1 https://www.dictionary.com/browse/socialism.

2 D. A. Carson, quoted in Stephen Beale, "The Deeper Meaning of the Story of Jesus and the Moneychangers," Catholic Exchange, February 13, 2017, https://catholicexchange.com/deeper-meaning-story-jesus-moneychangers/#:~:text=As%20one%20commentator%2C%20D.A.%20Carson,petition%2C%20there%20is%20noisy%20commerce.

3 Martin Luther King, Jr., "I've Been to the Mountaintop," speech delivered at Mason Temple, April 3, 1968, Memphis, TN, 32 min. 8 sec., audio recording provided by The Martin Luther King, Jr. Center for Nonviolent Social Change, https://www.youtube.com/watch?v=gC6qxf3b3FI&t=1928s.

4 Martin Luther King, Jr., "The Three Dimensions of a Complete Life," sermon delivered at New Covenant Baptist Church, April 9, 1967, Chicago, IL, 9 min. 26 sec., audio recording provided by The Martin Luther King, Jr. Center for Nonviolent Social Change, https://www.youtube.com/watch?v=GU3AnO_PJGU.

5 Martin Luther King, Jr., "The Three Dimensions of a Complete Life," sermon delivered at New Covenant Baptist Church, April 9, 1967, Chicago, IL, 11 min. 24 sec., audio recording provided by The Marting Luther King, Jr. Center for Nonviolent Social Change, https://www.youtube.com/watch?v=GU3AnO_PJGU.

6 Gore Vidal, https://quoteinvestigator.com/2014/09/11/friend-succeeds/.

7 https://www.dictionary.com/browse/socialism.

8 Lawrence W. Reed, "Rendering Unto Caesar: Was Jesus a Socialist?" Foundation for Economic Education, March 3, 2015, https://fee.org/ebooks/rendering-unto-caesar-was-jesus-a-socialist/#:~:text=The%20empirical%20evidence%20today%20is,economic%20growth%20and%20are%20more.

9 Lawrence W. Reed, "Rendering Unto Caesar: Was Jesus a Socialist?" Foundation for Economic Education, March 3, 2015, https://fee.org/ebooks/rendering-unto-caesar-was-jesus-a-socialist/#:~:text=The%20empirical%20evidence%20today%20is,economic%20growth%20and%20are%20more.

10 Chick-fil-A 140,000 team members, https://www.chick-fil-a.com/our-standards/taking-care-of-restaurant-team-members#:~:text=of%20our%20customers.-,Supportive%20Workplace,in%20the%20communities%20we%20serve.

11 Bono, as in David Marchese, "Bono Is Still Trying to Figure Out U2 and Himself, " New York Times Magazine, Oct. 24, 2022, https://www.nytimes.com/interactive/2022/10/24/magazine/bono-interview.html.

Fine Art Index

Fine Art Index Continued

Grace & Favor Publishing, a unit of the Job Creators Network, merges a passion for faith with the entrepreneurial spirit, offering resources that inspire spiritual growth while encouraging individuals to balance their faith and work.

Rooted in the conservative values championed by our parent organization, we recognize the transformative power of free enterprise and the opportunities it provides for individuals and families to thrive. Guided by the wisdom of Job Creators Network's mission to protect Main Street and support small businesses, Grace & Favor aims to equip readers not only with tools to deepen their connection to God but also with principles to navigate the challenges of work and life with integrity and purpose.

By fostering understanding and encouraging a commitment to faith-based living, we aspire to empower individuals to make a lasting impact in their communities and workplaces, reflecting the strength of a free-market economy and the enduring values it upholds.